The City Of Carcassonne

Viollet-le-Duc, Eugène-Emmanuel, 1814-1879

ALBERT MORANCÉ
PUBLISHER, PARIS
30-32, RUE DE FLEURUS

LATE FIRM MOREL
ESTABLISHED 1780

THE CITY

OF

CARCASSONNE

BY VIOLLET-LE-DUC, Eugène En

ÉDITIONS ALBERT MORANCÉ

45

THE CITY

OF

CARCASSONNE

HISTORY

About the year 636 of Rome, the Senate, on the advice of Lucius Crassus, having decided that a Roman colony shoud be established at Narbonne, the border of the Pyrenees was soon provided with important posts in order to keep the passages into Spain and defend the course of the rivers. The « Volces Tectosages », having opposed no resistance to the Roman armies, the Republic granted to the inhabitants of Carcassonne, Lodève, Nîmes, Pézenas and Toulouse, the privilege of governing themselves according to their laws and under their magistrates. The year 70 a. J.-C., Carcassonne was classed with cities said to be *noble* or *elected*. The fate of Carcassonne since then down to the fourth century is unknown. Like all the cities of Southern Gaul, it enjoyed profound peace, but, after the disasters of the Empire, it was only considered as a citadel (*castellum*). In 350 the Franks took it but, soon after, the Romans entered it again.

In 407 the Goths penetrated into the « Narbonnaise première », laid that province waste, passed into

Spain, and, in 436, Theodoric, king of the Visigoths, took Carcassonne. According to the treaty of peace which he concluded with the Empire in 439, he remained possessor of that city with all its territory, and the « Novempopulanie » situated to the West of Toulouse.

It is during that reign of the Visigoths that the inward city wall was built on the ruins of the Roman fortifications. And, in fact, most of the Visigoth towers still standing are laid upon Roman substructions which appear to have been built in haste, probably at the time of the Frank invasions. The bases of the Visigoth towers are square or have been roughly rounded off to sustain the defence-works of the Vth century.

On the Southern side of the city-wall we notice basements of towers built with enormous blocks laid over each other without any mortar and which belong certainly to the time of the Empire's decay. Whatever be the case it is still easy to-day to follow the whole wall of the Visigoths (See the general plan fig. 16 (1). That wall had an oval shape with a slight depression on the western side following the configuration of the hill on which it was built. The towers, separated by a space or about 25 to 30 metres, are outwardly cylindric, ending in a square inside the town and joined together by high curtains (fig. 1). The whole Visigoth construction is built in layers of ashlars, about 0 m. 10 or 0 m. 12 in height, with rows of large alternated bricks. Wide semi-circular bays are opened in the cylindric part of those towers, on the side looking

---

(1) Excavations have allowed us to trace the foundations of that wall on the points were it was destroyed at the end of the XIIIth century in order to increase the perimeter of the city.

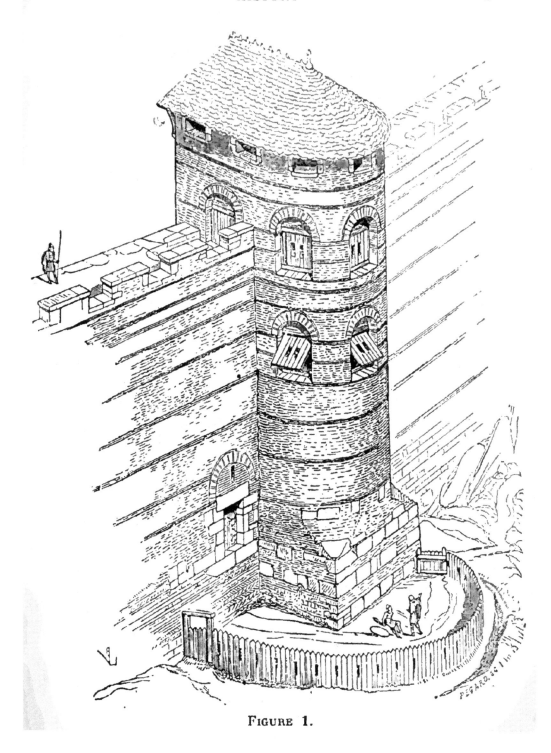

FIGURE 1.

to the country slightly above the level of the town; they were provided with wooden shutters with horizontal pivots and served as loop-holes. Those towers were crowned with covered battlements. From the curtain-watches the towers were reached through gate with lintels in the shape of surbased arches relieved by a semi-circular arch in brick. A wooden staircase inside made the lower story communicate with the higher battlements which opened towards the town by an arch pierced through the gable.

In spite of the modifications brought in the defence-system of those towers during the XIIth and XIIIth centuries, we still find all the traces of the Visigoth constructions. Down to the level of the ground of the curtain-watches those towers are entirely solid and thus present a powerful mass calculated to resist saps and batteringrams.

The Visigoths, among all the Barbarian peoples who invaded the East were those who assimilated most rapidly the remains of the Roman arts, at least with regard to military constructions and, indeed, those of Carcassonne are quite similar to those used about the end of Empire in Italy and in Gaul. They understood the value of the situation of Carcassonne and made it the center of their possessions in the Narbonnaise.

The table-land on wich the city of Carcassonne is built commands the valley of the Aude, which flows at the foot of the said table-land, and, consequently, the natural road from Narbonne to Toulouse. It rises between the Black Moutain and the slopes of the Pyrenees, precisely at the top of the angle formed by the river Aude on leaving those steep slopes to turn off towards the East. Carcassonne happens thus to bestride the only valley which leads from the Medi-

terranean to the Ocean, and is besides at the entrance
of the passes which penetrate into Spain through
Limoux, Alet, Quillan, Mont-Louis, Livia, Puicerda or
Campredon.—The seat of the city had thus been
perfectly chosen, and it had already been taken by
the Romans who, before the Visigoths, meant to
dispose of all the passages from the Narbonnaise into
Spain.

But the Romans found, via Narbonne, a shorter and
easier road to enter Spain and they had only made
Carcassonne a citadel (*castellum*) whereas the Visigoths, settling in the country after long efforts, probably preferred a place defended by nature and situated in the center of their possessions this side of the
Pyrenees to a town like Narbonne built on flat land,
difficult to defend and keep. Events proved that they
had not been mistaken; in fact Carcassonne was their
last refuge when they were in their turn, at war with
the Franks and the Burgundians.

In 508 Clovis laid siege to Carcassonne and was
obliged to break up his camp without having succeeded in taking the town.

In 588 the city opened its gates to Austrovalde,
duke of Toulouse, for king Gontran; but, soon after,
the French army having been defeated by Claude,
duke of Lusitania, Carcassonne fell again into the
power of Reccarede, king of the Visigoths.

It was in 713 that the kingdom ended; the Moors of
Spain then became possessors of Septimany. We can
only make vague conjectures as to what befell Carcassonne during four centuries; between the domi-
nation of the Visigoths and the beginning of the
XIIth century we find no certain traces of constructions in the city any more than on its walls. But, from

the end of the XIth century, important works were undertaken on several points. In 1096 the pope Urbain II came to Carcassonne to reestablish peace between Bernard Aton and the citizens who had rebelled against him and he blessed the cathedral (St-Nazaire) as well as the materials prepared to finish it. It is to that time indeed that the building of the nave of the church can be ascribed.

Under Bernard Aton the « bourgeoisie » of Carcassonne had formed a militia and peace does not seem to have reigned between that lord and his vassals, for the latter, beaten by the troops of Alphonse, count of Toulouse, who had come to Bernard's rescue, were obliged to submit and give warrants of their fidelity to find bail. The goods of the chief rebels were confiscated in favour of the few vassals who had remained loyal and Bernard Aton gave in fief to the latter the *towers* and houses of Carcassonne, on condition, says Dom Vaissette, « to keep watch and guard the city, some during four, the others during eight months of the year and to reside there all the while with their families and vassals. Those gentlemen, who called themselves lords of Carcassonne, promised by an oath to the viscount to keep the city faithfully. Bernard Aton granted them sundry privileges and they engaged in their turn to pay him homage and an oath of fidelity. That is what gave birth, it seems, to the « mortes-payes » of the city of Carcassonne, who are « bourgeois », who still have to keep the watch and enjoy therefore sundry privileges.

It was probably under viscount Bernard Aton or, at the latest, under Roger III, about 1138, that the castle was reared and the Visigoth walls repaired. The towers of the castle, by their construction and the few carvings which still decore the capitals of the small columns serving as mullions to the twin windows, certainly belong to the first half of the XIIth century. By going over the inner wall of the city we can easily mark out the parts of the buildings which date from that time; their kerb-stones are made of yellowish sandstone and set in layers of 0 m. 15 to 0 m. 25 in height by 0 m. 20 to 0 m. 30 in width and very roughly drafted.

On the first of August 1209 Carcassonne was besieged by the army of the crusader commanded by the famous Simon de Montfort.

Viscount Roger had had the defence-works of the city reinforced as well as those of the two faubourgs of Trivalle and Graveillant situated between the town and the river Aude, also towards the road to Narbonne.

The defenders, after losing the faubourgs, lacking water, were constrained to capitulate. The siege undertaken by the army of the Crusaders lasted only from the 10th to the 15th of August, the day of the surrender of the town. It cannot be admitted that during that short time the besiegers were able to execute the mining or sapping works which ruined part of the walls and towers of the Visigoths; the less so as there are underpinnings made during the XIIth century, to consolidate and raise the towers, which had been greatly damaged through sap and mine.

It must then be admitted that the siege-works and the breaks which are traced namely on the Northern side, are due to the Moors of Spain when they conquered that last bulwark of the Visigoth kings. Bernard Aton cannot be, either, the author of those mining-works, for the treaty which gave him back the city held by his rebellious subjects does not imply that he had to lay a long siege or that the defenders were reduced to the last extremity.

Viscount Bernard Aton, in defiance of the treaty which surrendered the city of Carcassonne to the Crusaders, had died imprisoned in one of the towers in November 1209. Since then, Raymond de Trincavel, his son, had been despoilt, in 1226, by Louis the VIIIth, of all his lands, reconquered over the Crusaders. Carcassonne was hanceforth part of the royal domain and a seneschal ruled it for the king of France.

In 1240, that young viscount Raymond de Toulouse, the last of the viscounts of Béziers, who had been put into the hands of the Count of Foix (he was then two years old) tuns up suddenly in the dioceses of Narbonne and Carcassonne with a body of troops from Catalonia and Aragon. He takes hold, without meeting any serious resistance, of the castles of Montreal, of the cities of Montolieu, Saissac, Limoux, Azillan, Laurens, and presents himself before Carcassonne.

There exist two versions of the siege of Carcassonne underkaten by young viscount Raymond in 1240, written by eye-witnesses : that of Guillaume de Puy-Laurens, inquisitor for the Faith in the region of Toulouse, and that of seneschal Guillaume des Ormes, who held the city for the king of France. The latter version is an account, in the form of a diary, addressed to Queen Blanche, the mother of Louis the IXth.

This important document explains to us all the dispositions of attack and defence ([1]). At the time of the

---

(1) The account of seneschal Guillaume des Ormes and the story of Guillaume de Puy-Laurens have been published and annotated by M. Douët d'Arcq, in the *Biblioth. de l'Ecole des Chartes*, 2º série, t. II, p. 363.

siege the walls of Carcassonne had neither the dimensions nor the strengh which were given them later on by Louis IX and Philip the Bold. The remains, still very obvious, of the wall of the Visigoths, repaired in the XIIth century, and the searches undertaken recently allow us to trace exactly the defence-works existing at the time when Raymond de Toulouse undertook to force them.

We give further on (fig. 2) the plan of those defence-works with the adjoining faubourgs, the barbicans and the course of the river Aude.

Trincavel's army invested the place on the 17th of September 1240 and got hold of the faubourg of Graveillant which was immediately retaken by the besieged. That faubourg, says the account is *ante portam Tolosæ*. Now the Toulouse-gate is no other than the gate called « de l'*Aude* » nowadays, which is a Romaïc construction bored into a Visigoth wall and the faubourg of Graveillant consequently can only be the faubourg called « de la *Barbacane* ». The sequel of the story shows us that this first surmise is accurate.

The besiegers were coming from Limoux, that is to say from the South; they had no need to cross the Aude before Carcassonne to invest the place. A stone-bridge existed over the Aude. That bridge still stands entire to-day, it is the old bridge « *le vieux pont* », the building of which dates partly from the XIIth century. It was only repaired and supplied with a bridge-head under Saint-Louis and Philip the Bold. It is under the letter P on our fig. 2.

Raymond de Trincavel was aware that the besiegers were expecting rescuers who could only rush into the city by passing the river Aude since they had to come from the North West. Therefore the viscount

took hold of the bridge, and, pursuing his attack
along the right bank of the river up the stream, be
tried to cut off the besiegers from every communication with the left bank.

Unable at first to maintain himself in the faubourg
of Graveillant (see fig. 2 : G), he takes hold of a fortified mill (M), on a branch of the Aude, sends off his
troops in that direction, lodges them in the lower
parts of the faubourg, and manages his attack in the
following way : part of the besiegers commanded by
Ollivier de Thermes, Bernard Hugon de Serre-Longue
and Giraud d'Aniort, camp between the North-Wes-
tern salient of the city and the river, dig trenches and
surround themselves with palisaded intrenchments.

The other body, headed by Pierre de Fenouillet,
Renaud de Puy and Guillaume Fort, is lodged before
the barbican B and that of the gate called Narbonnaise (N).

In 1240, besides those two barbicans, there existed
another : D (¹) which led down from te castle into the
faubourg (²) and yet another (H) facing the South.
The large barbican D also served to protect the Toulouse-gate T (to-day « porte de l'Aude »).

It must be noticed that the only points on which
the outward ground is nearly on the same level as the
lists (for Guillaume des Ormes points out the existence of the lists L and consequently of outward
walls), are the points O and R. As to the ground of
the barbican D in the castle, it was naturally on the
same level as the faubourg and consequently much
below the seat of the city. The whole western front

(1) Reconstructed under Saint-Louis.
(2) All the defence-works of the castle date from the XIIth century
except those of the South front.

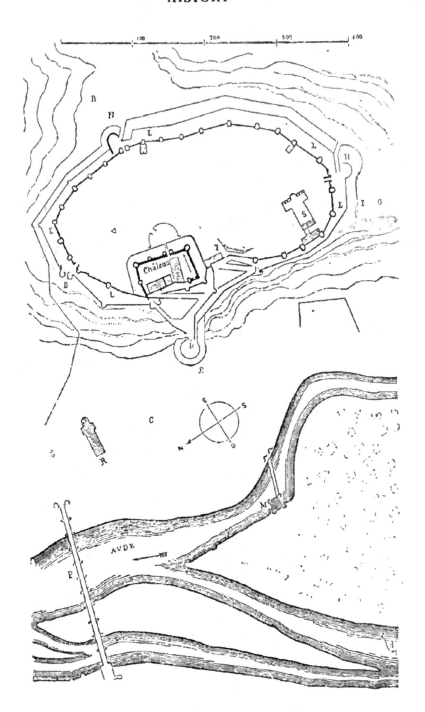

FIGURE 2.

of the city is built on a very high and steep escarpment.

On retaking at first the faubourg from the besiegers, the defenders of the city had hastened to carry into their walls a large quantity of wood which was very helpful to them; but they had to **give up the faubourg.**

The viscount then attacked at the same time the barbican D of the castle, to take from the besieged every chance of acting again on the offensive, the barbican B (it was, besides, a projection) the barbican N of the « Porte Narbonnaise » and the projection I on the level of the tableland which extended to a hundred metres on that side to the South-West.

The besiegers, camped between the city and the river were in a pretty bad position; they entrenched themselves therefore with great care and covered their fronts with such a great number of crossbowmen that no one could leave the town without getting wounded.

They soon reared a mangone before the barbican D.

The besieged, on their side, within the walls of that barbican, rear a Turkish « pierrière » ([1]) which batters the mangonel. To be as well defiladed as possible, the mangonel must have been set under the letter E.

Soon after, the besiegers began to undermine the barbican of the « porte Narbonnaise » (N) making their galleries start from the houses of the faubourg which on that side, nearly touched the defence-works.

The mines are propped up and shored with wood to which they set fire thus causing to fall part of the defence-works of the barbican.

[1] A machine to fling stones.

But the besieged have counter-mined in order to stop the progress of the enemy miners and have repaired the part of the barbican still standing. It is by mining-work that, on the two chief points of the attack, the men of the Viscount attempt to take the place. Those mines are pushed on with great activity; they are no sooner discovered than other galleries are begun.

The besiegers do not content themselves with those two attacks. While they batter the barbican D of the castle and ruin the barbican N of the Porte Narbonnaise, they endeavour to damage a part of the lists and engage in a very serious attack on the projection 1 between the bishop's palace and the cathedral of St Nazaire, marked S on our plan.

As we have already said, the table-land, on that point, extended almost on a level with the inside of the city from I to O, and that is why Saint Louis and Philip the Bold reared, on that table-land, outside the old Visigoth walls, considerable works, destined to command the escarpment.

The attack of Trincavel's troops is very sharply pursued on that side (a weak point then); the mines reach the foundations of the Visigoths walls, the shores are set on fire and ten fathoms of curtains crumble down. But the besieged have fortified themselves behind the breach with good palisades and « Bretèches (1) » so that the enemy troops dare not venture on an attack. Moreover mining-galleries are also opened before the Rodez-gate (B); the besiegers counter-mine and drive back the workmen of the besiegers.

Meanwhile, breaches had been opened on various

_____

(1) A small blockhouse made of timber.

points and Viscount Raymond, fearing to see at any moment the rescuers sent from the North turn up, decides to attempt a general attack. His men are driven back with considerable losses, and, four days later, hearing of the arrival of the royal army, he raises the siege after setting fire to the churches of the faubourg and among others, the church of the Minimes (R).

Trincavel's army had remained twenty-four days before the town.

Louis IX, laying great store by the place of Carcassonne, which covered that part of the royal domain before Aragon, and wishing to have to dread no longer the consequences of a siege which would have put it into the hands of an enemy always on the watch, decided to make it an impregnable fortress.

We must add to the story of Seneschal Guillaume des Ormes a fact related by Guillaume de Puy-Laurens. In the night of the 8th to the 9th of September, the inhabitants of the faubourg of Carcassonne (Trivalle: see the plan fig. 2), in spite of their vow of fidelity to the noblemen who held for the king, hat opened their gates to Trincavel's soldiers who, since then, directed from that faubourg an attack on the left, against the Porte Narbonnaise. Saint Louis, directly after the siege, was raised, had no need to destroy the « bourg » already burnt by Viscount Raymond, but, wishing on one hand to punish the inhabitants for their breach of faith, on the other to have to dread no longer a neighbourhood to dangerous for the city, he forbade the citizens of the faubourg of Graveillant to re-build their houses and had the faubourg of « la Trivalle » evacuated. Those unfortunate people had to go into exile.

Louis IX began immediately important works of
defence round the city; he had the remains of the faubourgs razed, cleared the ground between the city
and the bridge and reared all the outward walls which
we see today, so as to cover himself on all sides and
take time to improve the inward works. Enabled to
notice the weakness of the two parts of the walls
against which Viscount Raymond had rightly aimed
his two chief attacks, that is to say the south extremity and the Porte Narbonnaise, he extended the
outward walls far beyond the old south salient on the
table-land which commands, on that side, a ravine
opening into the Aude, about 30 metres to the outside,
thus locking in the new-works the two chief points of
Trincavel's attack (fig. 16).

Bent on making the city Carcassonne the bulwark
of that part of the royal domain against all attacks
from the heretic lords of the south provinces, saint
Louis would not permit the inhabitants of the old
faubourgs to re-build their dwellings in the neighbourhood of the city. At the prayer of Bishop Radulphe ([1]), after seven years of exile, he consented
only to allow those unfortunate refugees to settle on
the other bank of the river Aude. Here are saint
Louis's letters patent sent on that score ([2]) :

« Louis, by the grace of God, King of France, to
our friend and liege Jean de Cravis, seneschal of

(1) The tomb of that bishop is in the small chapel built at the
extremity of the south arm of the cross of the church of Saint-
Nazaire.

(2) *Hist. des Antiq. et comtes de Carcassonne*, G. Besse, citizen of
Carcassonne, Béziers, 1645. « Those letters, says Besse, were executed
by the seneschal, *pridie nonas Aprilis*, that is to say on the 4th of
April 1247 and, with the records of their execution, happen to have
been transcribed in the language of the country, in the manuscript-
book of the customs of Carcassonne. »

Carcassonne, greeting and love. We demand that you receive in safety the men of Carcassonne who had fled therefrom, because they had not paid to us the sums which they owed, after the payment of the said sums was due. As to the dwellings and habitations that they claim, you shall take advice and counsel of our friend and liege, the bishop of Carcassonne and of Raymond de Capendu and other good men, to grant them a place to inhabit provited no harm can come of it to our castle and city of Carcassonne. We wish you to give them back the property, inheritance and possessions which they enjoyed before the war and to let them enjoy their uses and customs so that we or our successors cannot change them. We mean, however that the said men of Carcassonne must re-make and build at their cost the churches of Notre-Dame and the Frères-Mineurs, which they had demolished; and, on the contrary, we mean that you shall in no wise receive any of those who introduced the Viscount (of Trincavel) into the « bourg » of Carcassonne, such being traitors. Therefore you shall recall the others who are not guilty. And you shall tell from us our frient and liege the bishop of Carcassonne, that he must renounce the fines which he claims from the fugitives, and of that we shall be grateful to him. Given at Helvenas, the Monday after St Peter's See (la chaise de Saint Pierre). »

Although we do not possess the original text of that piece, but only the transcription of it obviously altered by Besse, that document is no less very important in that it gives us the date of the foundation of the present city of Carcassonne. Indeed, in execution of those letters patent, the place to build the new bourg was laid out beyond the river Aude, and as that place belonged to the bishopric the king indemnified the bishop by giving him a half of the town of Villalier. The records of that exchange were noted down at Aigues-Mortes with the seneschal in August 1248.

That bourg is nowadays the city of Carcassonne, built at one cast, on a regular plan, with streets in straight rows, intersecting one another at right angle, a square in the centre and two churches.

The prudence of Louis IX did not confine itself to clearing the outskirts of the city and to rearing new outward walls; he built the big circular works called « the Barbican » instead of the one which commanded the faubourg of Graveillant. That faubourg, rebuilt later on, took its name from those warks.

He made that barbican communicate with the castle, by fortified inclined planes, very cleverly conceived in order to defend the place. From the manner in which the works of the outward walls are made we have reason to think that the building was pushed on actively in order to guard the city from a sudden attack, and to find time to repair and enlarge the outward walls.

Philip the Bold when at war with the king of Aragon continued those works with great activity. They were finished at the time of his death (1285). Carcassonne was the centre of the operations underkaten against the army of Aragon, and a safe shelter in case of failure.

In the place of the old gate called « Pressam » or « Narbonnaise », or « des Salins » Philip the Bold built admirable defence works including the present « Porte Narbonnaise », the « Trésau » tower, and the fine neighbouring curtains. On the west-south-west side, on one of the points most sharply attacked by Trin-

cavel's army, taking advantage of the salient which
St-Louis had had made, he rebuilt all the inward
works, that is to say, the towers n°ˢ 39, 11, 40, 41, 42,
43 (Gate of « Razez, St-Nazaire, or des Lices »), as
well as the high intermediate curtains (fig. 16), so as
to command better the valley of the river Aude and
the extremity of the tableland. A curious fact ascribes
a definite date to the part of the walls which surrounded the bishop's palace. In August 1280, at Paris.
king Philip allowed Isard, then bishop of Carcassonne, to open out four grated windows in the curtain
leaning against the palace, after taking the seneschal's advice and under the express condition that
those windows should be walled up in case of war,
reserwing to open them again at the end of the war.
The king bound himself to make, at his cost, the
sewers for the drainage of the waters of the palace,
through the wall, and the bishop was to keep posses-
sion of the stories of the tower called the Bishop's
tower (a square tower n° 11 bestriding the two walls),
up to the loop-holing, without prejudice to the other
rights of the bishop over the rest of the city-walls.
Now, those four windows have not been opened after-
wards, they were built on rearing the curtain, and
still exist between the towers n° 39, 11 and 40; consequently those curtains and towers date from 1280.
On the south and south east sides, Philip the Bold
had the Visigoth towers capped, raised and even
re-built on some points, as well as the old curtains. On
the north side the damaged parts of the old towers
were repaired and a large barbican reared before the
entrance of the castle inside the city.

The outward walls, which I consider as a few years
older than the reparations undertaken by Philip the

Bold, to improve the inward walls,—and I am going
to give certain proofs thereof,—are built of irregular
materials (sandstone) roughly disposed, but presenting level kerb-stones, whereas all the constructions
of the end of the XIIIth century have kerb-stones
chiselled on the arris and form a sort of rustic bosses
which impart to those constructions a robust and
very effective look. All the profiles of the towers of
the inner wall, repaired by Philip the Bold are exactly
alike; the pendants of the arches of the vaults and
the few rare sculptures such, for instance, as the
statue of the Virgin and the niche placed above the
« Porte Narbonnaise », undeniably belong to the end
of the XIIIth century.

In those constructions the materials are of the
same nature, coming from the same quarries and the
mode of draught being uniform; everywhere we come
across those bosses, as well in the entirely new parts,
like those of the west, the south-west and the east, as
in the portions which have been completed or restored on the Visigoth constructions and on those of the
XIIIth century. The mouldings are finely carved and
already meagre whereas the outer walls offers in its
loopholes, its gates and its corbels very simple and
broad outlines. The key-stones of the tower n° 18
(tower called de la Vade ou du Papegay) are decorated with sculptured figures presenting all the charac-
teristics of the imagery of St-Louis's time. Moreover,
between the tower n° 7 and the western watch-tower,
the parapet of the curtain has been raised, leaving
however the primitive merlons which are thus included in the higher masonry, so as to give to that curtain considered to be too low a wider outlook.

Now that superadded masonry is built in stones

with bosses, the battlements are more distant from each other, the draught much more careful than in the lower part and in everything absolutely like the draught of the 1280 structures. The difference between the two structures can be noticed by the most unpractised observer: Therefore the lower part being as to the mode of construction like all the rest of the outer wall and the higher part similar in draught to all the structures due to Philip the Bold, the outer wall has evidently been erected before the restorations and adjunctions undertaken by Louis the ninth's son.

On the south-west side, the wall of the Visigoths ran along the western front of the cathedral of St-Nazaire (fig. 16) that front, raised as we said at the end of the XIth century or at the beginning of the XIIth, is only a very thick wall without any opening in the lower part. It commanded the Visigoth wall and increased in strength on that vulnerable point, its coping consisted in battlements of which we have found the traces and which we have been able to reconstitue entirely. The fortifications of Philip the Bold allowed between themselves and that front (fig. 16) a very wide space and the upper defence-works of the « St-Nazaire » front remained purposeless since they in longer commanded the outworks. Since then no work of defence was undertaken in the city of Carcassonne and, throughout all the middle ages, that fortress was considered as impregnable; the fact is, it was never attacked and only opened its gates to the Black Prince Edward in 1355 when the whole region of « Languedoc » had submitted to that conqueror.

DESCRIPTION

OF THE

DEFENCE-WORKS OF THE CITY

I tried to give a very brief account of the history of the strutures which compose the walls of the city of Carcassonne, so as to explain to interested travellers the irregularities and differences in aspect shown by those works, which date in part from the Roman and Visigoth rule and which have been successively modified and restored, during the XIIth and XIIIth centuries by the viscounts and by the king of France. When we come to the city of Carcassonne, we are struck at once by the grand and severe aspect of those brown towers so varied in dimensions and shape and which follow, as well as the high curtains which join them, the undulations of the ground so as to obtain an outlook on the country and utilize as much as possible the natural advantages offered by the steeps of the tableland along which they have been reared. On the eastern side opens out the chief entrance, the only one accessible to carting : it is the « Porte Narbonnaise » defended by a ditch and a barbican supplied with loop-holes and battlements with a watch. The entrance is slant, so as to mask the gate of the chief work. The castle which can be isolated from the barbican, preceeds it, astride on the bridge which was composed of two sliding platforms the spindles of which are still in their places. That

4

barbican and the castle are opened at the gorge, so as to be battered by the upper work of the « Porte Narbonnaise » if those first structures fell into the enemy's power.

On the outward side the two huge towers, between which the gate opens, are reinforced by « becs », a sort of buttress meant to keep off the besieger from the tangent point the most assailable, to force him to unmask himself, to turn aside the battering ram (« bosson » in the oïl dialect) or to oppose a thicker masonry to the mine.

The entrance was closed, firstly by a chain, the fastenings of which are still in their places and which was meant to prevent the horses from rushing into the city. A machicoulis protects the first portcullis and the first wooden-gate with bars; in the vault opens a second machicoulis and a third is found before the second portcullis. It was not easy then to overcome all those obstacles but that entrance was defenred in a still more effectuad way in war-time.

Over the arch of the gate, on the two sides of the niche occupied by the statue of the Virgin, can be seen, on the flanks of the two towers, three neatly made notches; the two nearer the angle are cut square and 0 m. 20 in depth, the third is belleved, as if to hold the foot of a wooden rafter or of a slanting joist. Above the niche of the Virgin, we notice three other deep square holes meant to hold wooden pieces forming a strong jut. Those holes held indeed the wooden pieces of a penthouse forming a marked jut over the gate thus protecting the niche and the guardsmen at the entrance of the city.

That penthouse subsisted in peace-time; in war-time it served as machicoulis. At 1 m. 30 above the roofing of that penthouse can still be seen, on the flanks of the two towers, on each side, four notches or square holes, on the same level, the three first serving as props to the joists of the penthouse, and the fourth at 0 m. 60 in front.

There was set the floor of the second machicoulis. The fifth notch, cut between the two last and slightly above them, served as guard to hold the sliding madrier meant to protect the besieged against the projectiles flung up from the outside, and maintained, by a system of props, the whole of that upper story, thus keeping it from tumbling down; it was only possible to pass from the towers into those outer machicoulis through an opening contrived in the second story and by ladders, so as to isolate those machicoulis in case the besiegers should take hold of them. Those wooden works were protected by mantlets pierced with loopholes. The besieger, to be able to approach the first portcullis, was thus forced to face a shower of arrows and of projectiles flung from the three machicoulis two of these being set in war-time and the last being part of the very structure. Moreover the top of the towers was set with timber covings which were equally set in war-time (1). The holes destined to the passage of the sliding joists which supported those covings are all intact and disposed in such a way that, from the inside, it was possible, in a very short time, to set those wooden works, the covering of which was connected with that of the perma-

---

(1) The reader remembers that Seneschal Guillaume des Ormes congratulates himself for having been able to retake the « faubourg de Graveillant » in which was found a provision of wood which proved useful to the besieged.

nent coping. Indeed, it is easy to conceive that, with the system of battlements and of loopholes contrived in the cope-stones, it was impossible to prevent assailers numerous and bold, protected by shields and even by « chats » (a sort of chariot covered up with madriers and skins) from sapping the foot of the towers, since, from the loop-holes, in spite of the pronounced sloping of their plan it is impossible to see the foot of the towers or surtains and since, through the battlements, nuless a man threw half his body out of their joist, it was not possible either to aim at an object placed at the foot of the scarp.

It was then necessary to establish continous works, covered, and allowing a great number of defenders to batter the foot of the towers by flinging stones or projectiles of every description.

The plan (fig. 3), which we give here, made on the axle of the « Porte Narbonnaise », sets forth the dispositions which we have just sketched.

Not only did the covings fulfil that purpose, but they allowed the defenders full freedom in their movements the watchers inside the battlements being kept for gathering projectiles and circulating.

Moreover, if those covings were pierced with loopholes, besides the continuous machicoulis, the loopholes contrived in the stone-merlons remained unmasked in their lower part and allowed the crossbowmen, posted inside the parapet on that watch, to fling arrows at the assailers. The defence was thus as active as possible and a lack of projectiles alone would leave some respite to an attack.

We must not wonder, then, if, during some memorable sieges, after a protacted defence, the besieged were reduced to uncovering their houses, pulling

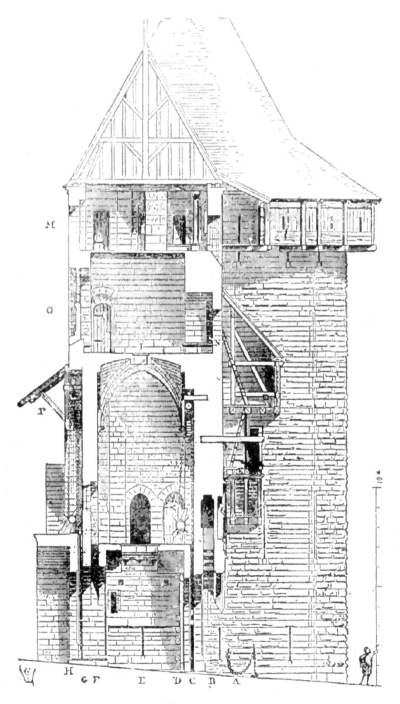

FIGURE 3.

down the garden-fences and unpaving the streets to supply the covings with projectiles and force the assailers to recede from the foot of the towers and walls.

On the other and, the besiegers tried to set fire to those wooden covings, which made the work of the sappers impossible or to break them by means of stones flung by the mangonels or the trebuchets, and it must not have been very difficult, especially when the walls were not very high. Therefore, as early as the end of the XIIIth century, they began to supply the walls and towers with stone-machicoulis resting on consoles such as can be seen at Beaucaire, Avignon and in all the castles or walls of the XIVth or XVth centuries (1).

At Carcassonne, the stone-machicoulis appears nowhere and everywhere, on the contrary, are found the holes of the wooden-covings, in the fortifications of the castle which date from the beginning of the XIIth century, as well as in the works of Louis the IXth and Philip the Bold.

In the XIIIth century, the Black mountain and the slopes of the Pyrenees were covered with forests; it was then easy to use largely those materials so common at the time in the region of Carcassonne.

The coping of the two walls of the city, curtains, and towers, are all pierced with those square holes crossing at equal distances the foot of the parapets on the level of the watches. The upper stories of the towers and large sheds built inside the curtains, as

(1) In the castle of Coucy, reared in the beginning of the XIIIth century, the stone-machicoulis already begins to replace the wooden covings. There we see already large stone-consoles support the wooden-coving.

FIGURE 4.

we shall explain presently, served to hold those pro-
visions of wood which were always to be ready to set
the town into a state of defence.

At ordinary times, the stone-coping could suffice
and we still see how, in the upper stories of the
towers, the battlements were supplied with shutters
with cylinders : sorts of ports moving on a wooden
axle set on two iron hooks; shutters which allowed
the besieged to see the foot of the ,walls without
unmasking themselves, and which sheltered the posts
of the upper stories from wind and rain. The lower
shutters were easily taken off when they set the
covings, for, then, the battlements served as communication between those covings and the watches or
the inside floors.

Our figure 4 explains the disposition of those shutters, the upper part turning upon two fixed hinges
remained, the lower part being taken off when they
set the covings.

But let us revert to the « Porte Narbonnaise ».
Besides, the chain (A) (Fig. 3) behind the first semi-
circular arch of the entrance, and between that arch
and the second, opens a machicoulis (B), through
which they flung the projectiles right and left at the
assailers who attempted to brake the first portcullis
(C). The reducts which held the defenders are defiladed by a thick parapet of stones, the working of the
portcullises is perfectly comprehensible still to-day.
In the wall which is above the entrance we notice in
the two first two pilasters of the groove of that first
portcullis the slanting notches which held the two
stanchions of the windlass sketched on our plan, and
the fastenings of the iron-links which maintained the
tops of those stanchions; on the level of the ground

the two holes destined to hold the wedges on which rested the portcullis when lifted; under the arch, at the top of the tympanus, the deep hole which held the suspension of the pulleys destined to the play of the counterpoises and of the chain wound round the windlass.

Behind the portcullis, there was a thick gate with two leaves (D) moving upon lower toadstones and pivots fixed in a wooden lintel, the fastenings of which are intact. Those leaves were strongly joined by a bar which jointed into the notch ready in the facing of the wall, on the right, when the gate was open, and by two other wooden bars fitting into some notches contrived in the two walls of the lobby.

If we get into the middle of the passage we see open in the vault a large square hole (E) which communicates with the hall of the first story. The extent of that hole is due to the necessity in which the besieged found themselves to fling projectiles not only in the middle, but also along the walls of the passage. The vault of the first story is equally pierced with a square hole (1) but smaller, so that from the second story it was possible to crush down the assailers, in case they should have taken hold of the lower hall, and also to give orders to the men who occupied it.

On the two sides of that large machicoulis, in the first story, there exist two deep reducts which could serve as refuge and defilade the defenders in case the assailers, masters of the passage, should have flung up arrows at them. Further, the width of that machicoulis made it possible to fling at the assailer burning fagots and the reducts thus sheltered the defender against flame and smoke while leaving them the

5

means of feeding the fire. Lateral loop-holes, pierced in the passage on the level of the ground (E), allowed the cross-bowmen, posted in the ground-floor halls of the two towers, to fling tiles point blank at the men who might dare to venture between the two porte-cullises.

As well as before the outward portcullis (C) there exist in the hall of the first story a second oblong machicoulis (F) destined to protect the second portcullis (J). This machicoulis was closed, as well as the opening contrived in the vault of the passage, by a trap-door, the grooves of which, cut in the wall, still exist. By means of a small window which lighted the hall of the first story, the besieged, from inside, could communicate orders to those who held the portcullis on the watch contrived over the second gate (H). That second portcullis worked under an arch reserved to that effect; its wind-glass was moreover protected by a penthouse (P) maintained by strong iron-hooks which are still sealed in the wall. The whole play of that portcullis is still visible; its iron work is still in its place, the portcullis alone is lacking.

The two towers which flank that entrance are laid out in the same way. They include : A story of cellars dug under the ground. The ground-floor pierced with loop-holes and vaulted with four staircases to communicate with the first floor; the first floor equally vaulted, pierced with loop-holes and provided with two chimneys and two kilns. Two of the staircases only go up to the upper floor, the two others do not reach there and can thus mislead people who should not know the precints. A second story was formely covered by a floor leaning on the border of the watch;

that second story is pierced, on the side of the city, with rich gothic windows wich mullions (O) which opened only in the lower part of the shutters, whereas the pannels of the windows were glazed up; those windows were strongly grated outside. A third embattled story held the timber of the covering; that timber divides into three pavilions, two over the two towers and one intermediate pavilion above the gate. At the time of the first construction, reconstituted nowadays, those three pavilions at the point of their intersection, were supported by rafters fitting into notches contrived in the layer of the cornice; whether those rafters gave way, or whether the waters of the badly kept gutters made them rot, in the XVth century, that covering was repaired and, to support it, they reared two large arches which fitted very badly with the structure of the XIIIth century, since one of them tumbled into one of the battlements and closed it up. The stone gutters were set on those arches and held the feet of the coping of the roofs at the points of their junction. Projecting gurgoyles threw out the waters of the gutters on the country-side. Those arches which drove out the large wall erected on the side of the city had to be taken off.

The watch of the curtain is not broken off by the « Porte Narbonnaise » according to the ordinary system adopted in the defence-works of that period. It passes, on the side of the city, over the gates, and connects the two curtains in such a way, however, that it communicates with the city only by the inside staircases of the towers and by a single bay formerly closed by two thick iron-bound leaves. The present staircase which gives access to that watch is modern, and has been built by military engineers.

Usually the towers of the inward wall, and even of the outward wall, break off the watches; so that, if the assailer should succeed in getting hold of the curtain, he would be caught between two towers and, unless forcing the ones after the others, it became impossible for him to go freely around the ramparts; the more so as the staircases, which set the watches in direct communication with the terre-plein on the city-side, are very few, and it is only possible to go up to those watches by ascending the staircases contrived in the towers. Thus each tower was a separate reduct independent and to be forced. The gates which made the towers communicate with the watches are narrow, strongly iron-bound, barred inside, so that in a moment it was possible to close the leaf and barricade it by drawing swiftly the wooden bar set in the wall before even taking time to push the bolts and turn the key. Careful examination of those works brings out the precautions taken by the engineers of the tower against surprises. All sorts of measures have been taken to stop the enemy and worry him at every step by unexpected contrivances. Evidently, a siege at that time became serious for the besieged, as well as for the assailer, only when they had come to fight, so to speak, hand to hand. A warlike garrison could struggle with good chances even in their last defence works. The enemy entered the city by scaling the wall or through a breach, without forcing the garrison to surrender, for, then, the besieged, shut up in the towers, which are, I repeat, so many independent reducts, could still defend themselves; barricaded gates had to be forced. Should the groundfloor of a tower be taken, the upper stories kept the means of taking the offensive again and crushing the enemy.

We see that every thing was calculated for a possible foot by foot struggle. The spiral staircases were easily barricaded, so as to render futile the efforts of the besieger to reach the upper stories.

Should the « bourgeois » of the city wish to surrender, the garrison defended themselves against them and forbade them access to towers and curtains. It was a system of defiance driven to the extreme.

The flinging-machines, the engines which the assailers had at their disposal, then, to batter from the outside walls like those of the city of Carcassonne, could produce only a very small effect, owing to the strength of those works and the thickness of the merlons; for the firing artillery alone could damage them. There were left the sap, the mine, the battering-ram and all the engines which forced the assailer to go up to the very foot of the defence-works.

Now, it was difficult to stand and sap under those powerful covings which hurled projectiles. The mine was not much good here for all the walls and towers were set on the rock.

We must not be surprised if, in those distant times, certain sieges lasted indefinitely. The city of Carcassonne was, at the end of the XIIIth century, with its double walls and ingenious contrivances of the defence, an impregnable place which could only be reduced by famine and, even then, to invest it, a numerous army would have been needed, for it was easy for the garrison to keep the banks of the Aude by means of a large barbican (N° 8 of the plan fig. 16) which allowed the besieged to sally forth in imposing numbers and hurl back the besiegers into the river.

On examining the general plan we see at the foot of the escarpment of the city, before the towers

11 and 12 in the west, a wall which defended the « faubourg de la Barbacane ». That wall dates from the XIIIth century, and it was certainly reared to prevent the enemy from posting themselves, as Trincavel had done, between the river Aude and the city. That wall is within crossbow range of the towers 11, 12 and 40 and is commanded by these. It was therefore very difficult to reach the barbican by going down the right bank of the Aude in spite of the garrison of the city.

The ramparts and towers present a formidable look especially on the points of the walls which are comparatively easily approched, wherever natural escarpments do not oppose a powerful obstacle to the assailer. On the north-east east and south sides, where the table-land on which the city is set is about on the same level as the country, large ditches protect the first walls. It is probable that the extremities of those ditches as well as the outposts of the gates, were defended by outward blockades according to the custom of the time. Those blockades were procided with opening fences.

On advancing in the lists, between the two walls, the first tower we see on the right after the « Porte Narbonnaise ».is the tower n° 21 called « du Treshaut », or « du Trésau », « de Tressan », « du Trésor » or « de la Cendrino ». That structure is a magnificent work of the end of the XIIIth century, contemporary of the « Porte Narbonnaise ». It commands the whole country the town, and, reaching almost to the outward walls, it commanded the table-land, the barbican of the « Porte Narbonnaise » and prevented the enemy to spread on the northside in the lists along which stand the Visigoth towers.

DESCRIPTION OF DEFENCE-WORKS

The tower « du Treshaut », besides it cellars, includes four stories, two of which are vaulted.

The lower story is dug underneath the « terre-plein » of the town. The second story is almost on the same level as the inward ground of the town. The third story was covered with a floor and the fourth, under covering, on the level of the battlement-watch.

The watch of the curtains passes behind the gable of the tower, but has no communication with the inward halls.

On the town side, the upper part of the tower ends in an embattled gable with rampant staircases along the covering. Two square towers, provided with staircases and embattled in their lower part, support the gable and served as watch-towers, for they are, on that side, the highest point of the works.

In peace-time, the battlements of the « Tour du Treshaut » were not covered. The covering rests on an inward wall. The gurgoyles which still exist inside show in a certain way that the upper watch was under open sky. In war-time the roofing of the covings covered those watches as well as the covings themselves.

A single spiral staircase does duty for the first stories, and all the issues were provided with strongly iron-bound gates. The second story over the cellars contains a small room, or reduct lighted by a window destined to the captain, a large chimney, and water-closets; that story and the ground-floor are pierced with numerous loop-holes opening under big arches provided with stone benches. The loop-holes are not pierced one above the other but overlap, « vides sur pleins » so as to batter all the points of the circumference of the tower. That principle is generally followed in the towers of the inwards valls and without exception in the towers of the outward wall, where the loop-holes play an important part. Indeed, the loop-holes pierced in the stories of the towers could serve only when the enemy were still far from the ramparts; we understand, then, why they have been contrived in greater number and disposed with more method in the towers of the outward walls.

The curtains which belong to the « tour du Treshaut » are very fine. Their lower part is pierced with loop-holes on level with the « terre-plein » of the town under semi-circular arches with stone-benches, and their merlons, wide and thick, are well built.

The inward facing of the merlons between the « tour Narbonnaise » and the « tour du Treshaut » is not vertical, but sloping. The disposition of the covings explains the use of that inclination of the inward facing of the merlons.

On that point of the defence-work — one of the most assailable, on accrount of the table-land which extends on a level before the « Porte Narbonnaise » — the inward curtains must have been provided with those double covings which are sometimes mentioned in the chronicles of the XIIIth century (1).

(1) At Toulouse, besieged by Simon de Montfort, the inhabitants strengthen incessantly the defences of the city :

« E parec ben a lobra e als autres mestiers
« Que de dins et defora ac aitans del obriers
« Que garniron la vila els portals els terriers,
« Els murs et las bertrescas els cadafalcs dobliers
« Els fossatz e las lissas els pons els escaliers
« E lains en Toloza ac aitans carpentiers. »

Those « cadafalcs dobliers » are double covings. See « Poème de la Croisade contre les Albigeois », Collection of the unpublished documents of the history of France.

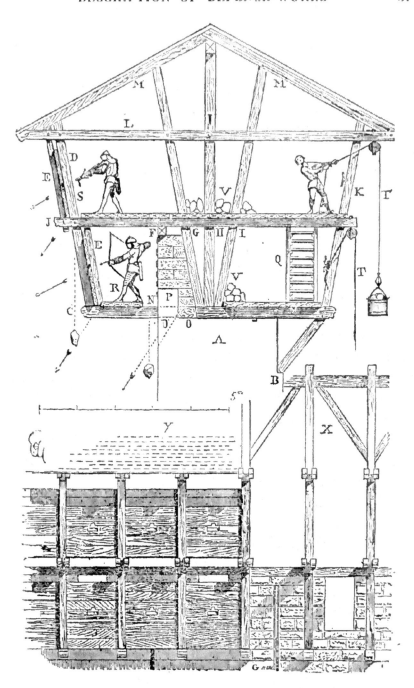

FIGURE 5.

The figure 5 explains in the present case the disposition of those double covings. As we have just said, the merlons having their inward facing sloping on the watch (A) their base is pierced on the level of that watch with coving holes 1 m. 30 in length at regular distances. On the facing of the watch, on the townside, is a continous set-back (B). The double covings, then, were disposed thus : every five feet passed through the coving-holes strong rafters (C), on the extremity of which, on the outside, stood the sloping post (D) with counter-posts (E) forming the groove for the passage of the madriers. Double braces (J) pinched that post (D), rested upon the joist (F), bit into the three posts (G, H, I), G being supported by the sloping facing of the merlon, and caught the hind post (K), equally inclined. A second row of braces (L) at 1 m. 80 from the first row, made drag of the cross-bowmen (M) of the coving. A machicoulis (N) was reserved along the outward facing of the curtain. That machicoulis was served by men posted (O) on the watch, on the right of each battlement provided with a joist (P). The archers and cross-bowmen of the lower coving were posted on the point (R) and were not needed to serve that first machicoulis.

The second coving possessed a machicoulis (S.). The stores of projectiles were got inside the town by the windlasses (T). Staircases (Q), disposed from place to place, made the two covings communicate. In this way it was possible to gather a considerable quantity of stones on the point (V), without hindering the circulation on the watches, nor the cross-bowmen at their posts. On the point (X), we see, in front, at the outside, the timber of the coving devoid of its madriers and, (on Y), that same timber provided with these. Through the loop-holes and machicoulis, it was thus possible to fling at the assailer a prodigious number of projectiles. As usual, the loop-holes U, pierced in the merlons, cleared the space under the covings and allowed a second row of cross-bowmen posted between the trusses, on the watch, to aim at the enemy.

We see that the inclination of the madriers was very favourable to the shooting. It permitted, moreover, to make the second machicoulis S slope outside the lower coving.

The expense necessitated by such considerable timber allowed only to set them under exceptional circumstances, on the points badly defended by nature.

The curtain which connects the « tour du Trésau » with the « porte Narbonnaise » possesses a small well and a flanking watch-tower destined to batter the interval between the barbican and that gate.

From the « tour du Trésau », on going northward, we walk along a large part of the Visigoth walls. Seeing the disorder of those old constructions, we must admit that they have been upset by a terrible siege; it is difficult to conceive how they managed, with the means they had at their disposal then, to pull down enormously thick bits of wall, bend those towers, the lower part of which offers one mass of masonry. It would seem that gun-powder alone could work such havock, and yet the siege, during which a considerable part of those ramparts has been pulled down, is previous to the XIIth century, since, on those ruins, we see arise constructions exactly like those of the castle, dating from the XIIIth century.

Scarcely did they trouble to clear the remains, for

we notice, locked in the curtains taken up in the
XIIIth century, enormous pieces of wall thrown down
and offering vertically the rows of their layers in
rough stone or brick. Tanks to the sound quality of
the mortars, those masses thrown down have not
fallen to pieces and stand there like rocks upon
which new walls might have been reared.

On that side, the curtains and towers are very high
and largely dominate the outward walls erected on
the crest of the escarpment.

That escarpment faces the river Aude and extends
up to the tower n° 41 which terminates the west
salient of the city.

Two gates are pierced in the walls of the Visigoths :
one, small, dating from the primitive period, has been
walled up; it is set on the right of the tower n° 26;
the other, pierced in the XIIth century and repaired
in the XIIIth, stands between the towers 24 and 25. It
is the gate which Seneschal Guillaume des Ormes
calls « porte de Rodez ». It offers no special defence,
but must have been preceded by a structure with a
postern, protected by the barbican-tower n° 4; a tower
which has been, unfortunately, modified in its shape
by the military engineers so that, to-day, the « porte
de Rodez » opens out into the lists and has no more
communication with the outside.

If we pass on to the other side of the castle, to the
south-west, we come across the « porte de l'Aude »
(formerly « porte de Toulouse »).

This gate was pierced in the Visigoth wall during
the XIIth century. We see, still, outside, the semi-
circular arch which seems to belong to that time,
from its draught and the materials employed. On the
left of that gate existed, on a Visigoth bif of wall, a

structure contemporary with the castle, that is to say erected during the XIth or XIIth century. The outward wall of that construction is still pierced with three little twin windows divided by small columns in marble with sculpted capitals.

A long ramp reached up to the large barbican n° 8 and was battered by that barbican; it rises, following a rather steep inclination, and, winding, leads up to a first gate, a simple fence defended by battlements and commanded by a big structure, built as a crossbar, ending, at the level of the watches of the outward wals, by a platform and some merlons. At its base, that cross-bar is pierced with a gate which opens out into the south-west lists.

It is necessary to ascend, inside the outward walls, a rather steep slope battered by the work which masks the « porte de l'Aude », pierced in the outward wall. That slope is commanded by the « Tour de la Justice » n° 37, and by a Visigoth tower, n° 38. A winding is thus reached which compels the comer to turn off suddenly to reach the gate. Although there are, in front of that gate, neither ditch nor weigh-bridges, it wass not easy to reach it, in spite of the people inside the town, for the space incluted between the two walls forms a regular parade, a large castle, commanded on every side, by formidable works. Moreover, the lists, right and left, were closed in by gates. It will be noticed that the upper gate is pierced in an inward angle, which permitted to flank it very powerfully, and, further, that its cast forms, in front, a small castle which could be closed entirely in war-time, and which, in peace-time, was preceded by a small post, the trace of which we still perceive along the curtain. From that structure the rounds could go

down into the south-west lists, by opening a gate
pierced on the flank of the parapet, and by setting
sliding-boards on the corbels fitted into the big
counterforts further on. That means of going out or
coming in shows well enough that the works, in front
of the « porte de l'Aude », were completely closed in
war-time.

On going from the « porte de l'Aude » to the south-
west lists, we soon leave the last traces of the Visigoth
constructions and reach the salient reared by Philip
the Bold, outside the grounds of the bishop's palace
(fig. 16). Having passed the gate pierced in the
commanding cross-bar which we believe to be the gate
called « du Sénéchal », we see one of the Visigoth
towers, entire, then the tower 39, called « de l'Inquisition » and in which we found a prison with a central pillar provided with chains, then the square
tower n° 11, called « de l'Evêque ». That tower,
astride over the lists, commands the two walls and
could, on that front, cut off all communication
between the south and the north part of the lists.
Howewer, the two arches thrown across the passage,
were only defended by two inward machicoulis and by
another pierced in the middle of the vault. We find
no trace of hinges showing the presence of gate-leaves,
but only notches, which lead us to suppose that, in
war-time, wooden-fences closed up those openings and
intercepted all communications. That tower of which
the bishop had the enjoyment, except the upper watch
is very fine, admirably built, proudly set on two walls,
breaking the uniformity of these. Besides cutting off
the communication with the lists, it also interrupted
the upper watch of the curtains, for, to go from the
north curtain to the south curtain, it was necessary

to go through that tower and force two gates. The inward staircases are contrived so as to make access to the battlements independent from access to the two vaulted halls, of which the bishop hod the enjoyment.

The curtains which make part of the salient built by Philip the Bold, are provided with fine loop-holes pierced under arcades with benches; loop-holes which batter the lists and the watches of the outward walls. We see further, outside that part of the outward walls, besides the tower n° 12, called « du Grand-Canisou », the apertures of the sewer which the king had had built through the wall reared at his order, to throw out the waters of the bishop's palace as was said before.

As to the structures of the bishop's palace, they are completely razed; such is not the case with the cloister of the church of St-Nazaire, the foundations of which have been found. Those foundations, and a wail of that cloister preserved, with the pillars engaged and the supporting arches of the vaults, are in keeping with the sketches of the old plans of the city, in which that cloister and its dependences are indicated. That structure dates from saint Loui's time. After the tower n° 11 stands the tower n° 40, called « de Cahusac » which offers a curious disposition : The watch winds around it ands is covered with a portico; then you arrive at the corner tower n° 41, called « Mipadre » or « de Prade ». It includes two vaulted stories and two stories between floors, it is provided with a chimney and a kiln. The only gate giving entrance into that tower, which does not break off the watch, is pierced on the east-side, and was locked by bolts and by a bar fitting into the wall. Just as is the other towers of that part of the walls, the last merlon of the curtains rises at the point of junction with the tower, where the gates are pierced, and the last battlement was equally provided with shutters on rollers, so as to protect those coming in and going out or the watchmen posted at the entrance of the towers. There are nearly always a few steps to be ascended to pass from the curtains into the towers, and then the battlements follow the slope.

It will be observed that the watches of the curtains, and consequently the battlements and the covings are not always on a level, but follow the slope of the outward ground so as to keep on all the points of the walls a uniform height in the escarpment, as is still done nowadays.

It was a rule established by experience, and, beyond a certain level, the scaling must be considered as impossible; therefore they maintained everywhere a minimum of elevation. However the escarpments of the inward walls are much higher than those of the outward walls. The outward walls were set so as to batter the assailer at great distance and prevent him from approaching; while, for the inward walls, everything is combined to fight a foe quite near. It is no use insisting on a disposition suggested by simple common sense.

Within the cloister St-Nazaire, large staircases give access to the ramparts. But it is good to observe that the cloister and the bishop's palace were already enclosed within walls and that, in consequence, the inhabitants of the town could not ascend from the public way to the curtains. Wherever there exist staircases ascending directly to the watches, those staircases are always either locked in old buildings dependent on the walls and fortified, or included within special walls; such are the staircases which went up to the curtain besides the tower n° 44, along the tower n° 47 and near the chapel Saint-Sernin (tower 53). Usually, it is the tower-staircases which, by means of small strongly iron-bound gates, give access to the watches. The garrison could, then, if they liked, as we said before, isolate themselves and keep the citizens in awe while they drove back the assailers. They alone went round the two walls; between the lists, while locking the gates of the town to the inhabitants; on that point there was no disadvantage to the watches being on a level with the « terre-plein ».

Following the inward walls towards the east, after passing the tower n° 42—called « tour du Moulin » because its upper story, in set back on the battlements, used to be affected to the mechanism of a windmill— you arrive at the tower n° 43, called « tour et posterne Saint-Nazaire ». That structure, on a square plane, is still one of the most remarkable of the city. Besides the barbican n° 15, called « de la Crémade » and dependent on the outward walls, is a low and narrow postern, opening into the ditch which is shallow on that point. That postern, in case of a siege, could be easily walled up, since it was sufficient to stop the steep staircase which, from the threshold of that postern, ascends to the lists. The large diameter of the « tour de la Crémade » makes it a barbican fitted, besides, to protect men going out or coming in. That tower was not covered, like the others, by a coving, and communicates directly with the watch of the curtains, of which it is only, so to say, a flanking appendage.

As to the « tour Saint-Nazaire », it was impossible for besiegers, posted outside the outward walls, to

7

suppose that it was provided with a postern. The gate
pierced at the foot that tower « Saint-Nazaire » and
opening into the lists is open on one side, masked by
the salient of the angle-watch-tower, and the threshold
of that opening is set at more tham two yards above
the ground of the lists. It was then necessary to set
ladders or a wooden inclined plane to get in and out.

In the tower itself the entrance is slanting, and if
from the outside you get in, through the postern pierced on the east flank, only my means of ladders or a
sliding floor, you can go through the second entrance
only by turning off at a right angle. Each postern, then,
could only be used by men on foot. Each of the two
bays is provised with portcullises, machicoulis and
leaves. A well does duty fort the lists and the first story
which also possesses a kiln. The first portcullis was
worked from the first story-hall, the second from the
watch as was the case at the « Porte Narbonnaise ».
The upper battlements are reared on a platform fitted
to receive a defensive-engine (mangonel) and have a
« guette » [1] for that point is one of the highest of the
city. The lower battlements (for the coping-defence is
double), is flanked by watch-towers which rise from
the foundations.

Still going eastward, we arrive, near the « tour Saint-
Nazaire », at the towed n° 44, called « Saint-Martin »,
which seems to have been reared in the neighbourhood
of the tower n° 43 on purpose, in order to mask and
batter the postern within a very short range. That
tower is reinforced, like the towers 41 and 42, and like
those of the « Porte Narbonnaise », by a projecting bec
the use of which we have explained. It includes two
vaulted stories, two stories under ceiling, like the

[1] An opening shaped as a half cross.

tower n° 41, and rises above the watch which winds round it on the townside.

From that point of the ouward walls, we see reappear in the lower parts of the curtains and towers, the remains of the Visigoth, ramparts down to the tower n° 53, called » de Saint-Sernin », besides the « Porte Narbonnaise ».

The towers n°ˢ 45, 46, 47, 49, 50, 52 and 53 are built on the foundations of the primitive towers and are of a smaller diameter than the towers of the XIIIth century. The tower n° 48 alone has been entirely re-built by Philip the Bold. In consequence, it presents, on the outside, a projecting bec, and its structure is very thick. That is because it was to rise high enough to command the tower n° 18 of the outward walls a tower called « de la Vade » or « du Papegay », a sort of projecting dungeon, absolutely independent and which was meant to batter the table-land that extends on a level, opposite to that front.

The preceding towers, n°ˢ 45, 46, 47, 49, 50 and 52, are not vaulted and wooden-ceilings separeted their stories two in number only, and set on the full ground-work of the Visigoth masonry. Their spiral staircases project inside the halls and take from the space of these. All those towers break off the circulation on the watch of the curtains; it is necessary to go through them to pass from one curtain into another. The tower n° 49, called « de Daréja », is built on a Roman substruction, made of big blocks of stone, perfectly adjusted, without any mortar. The Roman basement certainly supported a square tower, for the Visigoths contented themselves with hammering down the projecting arrises, in order to round off that massive structure which contains only on rubble.

On examining the constructions raised in the XIIIth century, we see that the engineers have given to the cylindric part (outward side) considerable thickness, while, on the town-side, where the tower is closed by a gable, the walls are pretty thin so as to obtain the greatest empty space possible inside to lodge watch-men. The tower n° 47 also presents, on the lists, in its lower part, the remains of Roman basements, on which is planted a Visigoth tower coped by the XIIIth century structure. Thus, all that part of the walls, included between the tower n° 44, and the « Porte Narbonnaise » has been repaired and re-built in part by Philip the Bold on the Visigoth walls, which had been reared on the Roman ramparts. The perimeter of the old town, then, is given by that of the Visigoth town since, on the south side as on the north side, we find the traces of Roman constructions under the works due to the Barbarians.

On all that south-east front, the covings presented in war-time and uninterrupted line, for those of the curtains are connected with those of the towers by means of a few steps. That was necessary to facilitate the defence and could have no disadvantages, in case when the besieger should have taken hold of part of those covings, for it was easy to cut them off in a moment and prevent the enemy from taking advan-tage of that outward continuous watch to take hold successively of the higher stories of the towers. The besieger, compelled to give up part of those covings, could set fire to them themselves, sacrifice, if neces-sary, one tower or two, and retire into the distant posts from the point fallen into the enemy's power, by cutting off the wooden-floors behind them.

The stone-tables of the watches of the curtains

reared under Philip the Bold are supporter inside, to increase the width of the upper watch, on the south and south-east sides, from the bishop's tower to the « Porte Narbonnaise », by stone-corbels. There exist between those corbels square holes very deep, contrived in the construction at equal intervals. Those holes were meant to hold horizontal joists the extremity of which could, if needful, be sustained by posts. On those joists was set a continuous floor which widener by so much the watch inside and formed a salient very useful to get stores for the covings, to put in battery stone-engines and trebuchets, and to dispose at the foot of the ramparts, on the « terre-plein » of the town stores and shelters for a supplement of garrison.

The roofings which covered the covings must very probably have covered also that supplement of watches. We see how those large spaces, contrived in the upper part of the curtains must have helped the defence. And it must be noted here that that disposition exists only in the part of the works which was least defended by the nature of the ground and against which, in consequence, the assailer must aim all his efforts and could organise a regular attack.

Those precautions would have been useless where the enemy could present themselves only in small numbers owing to the steeps of the hill. On the south side the enemy, supposing he had taken hold of the outward walls, could fill up part of the ditches, destroy a bit of the outward walls and drag near the inward walls, on an inclined plane, one of those timber-belfries, covered with fresh skins to ward off fire, by means of which assailers rushed directly on to the upper watches. It was only possible to resist such an attack which succeeded many a time, by gathering on the point assailed a number of soldiers superior to the besieging forces. How could they have done so on those narrow watches? The coving once broken, the merlons damaged by the stone-engines, the besiegers rushing on to the watches, found before them only a row of defenders brought to bay against an abyss and presenting only a shallow, line to that attacking-column ceaselessly renewed. With that supplement of watch which could be widened at will it was possible to oppose to the assailers a strong resistance, to hurl them back and even get hold of the belfry.

It is in those details of the foot by foot-defence that we see appear the art of fortification from the XIth to the XVth century. On examining carefully, on studying scrupulously and in the the smallest details, the defensive works of those times, we understand those tales of gigantic attacks which we are too ready to tax with exageration. Before means of defence so shrewd, so ingeniously combined, we find it easy to imagine the huge labours of the assailers, the sliding belfries, the stockades and castles with platforms, the revolving sapping-engines, such as « chats » and galleries, those mining-works which demanded considerable time, when gun-powder was not used by armies. With a resolute garrison, well provided, it was possible to make a siege last indefinitely. Therefore it is not uncommon to see a bit of a fortress resist for months to a numerous army. Thence, often, that recklessness and insolence of the weak towards the strong and powerful, that habit of individual resistance which was at the bottom of the character of feudal times, that energy which produced such great things and such great intellectual development amidst so many abuses.

Apart from the gates pierced in the inward walls there were several posterns. For the service of the besieged,—especially if they had to guard double walls—, it was necessary to make communications easy between those two walls and to contrive posterns opening out on the outside in order to be able to bring swift help on to a point attacked and to get bodies of men in and out without any possible opposition from the enemy. On going over the inward walls of Carcassonne, we see a large number of posterns more or less well concealed and which must have allowed the garrison to spread in the lists through a great number of issues easily masked, or to get in rapidly in case the first walls should have been forced. Between the « tour du Trésau », on the north side and the castle, we find two of those posterns, without counting the « porte de Rodez ». One of those posterns opens out into the ditch of the castle (fig. 16), the other besides. the tower n° 26. Between the castle and the tower n° 37 exists a postern equally opening out into the ditch of the castle. Between the « porte de l'Aude » and the « porte Narbonnaise » (west and south side of the outward walls) we find the postern « Saint-Nazaire » described before; between the towers 43 and 45, a postern communicating with a spiral staircase, and between the towers 50 and 52, a salient structure n° 51, which contained a wooden staircase, communicating with vast caves the outer issue of which is placed besides the tower of the outward walls n° 19, on the level of the bottom of the ditch and two galleries of those caves opened out into the lists. That last postern was very important for it made the upper watches communicate directly either with the lists or the outside. Therefore, behind the gate opening in the angle of the tower 19, is a vast vaulted hall capable of holding about forty armed men.

Besides, there exists a postern which makes the lists communicate with the ditch, at the intersecting angle formed by the curtain on the right and the dungeon « de la Vade » n° 18. There used to be a postern on the right side of the big tower n° 4 of the outward walls, a postern largely raised above the escarpment, pierced in the outward walls of the « Porte de l'Aude » and which required the use of a ladder, and the postern still open in the angle of the tower n° 15, as has been said before. Adding to those issues the large barbican of the castle n° 8 we see that the garrison could sally forth and communicate with the outside without opening the two chief gates « de l'Aude » and « Narbonnaise ».

Before we pass on to a description of the castle, it is necessary to speak of the outward walls which also offer considerable interest.

In those outward walls the best preserved tower (it is intact except for the covering) is that of « la Peyre » n° 19. That tower, like most of those dependent on those walls, is open on the town-side in the upper part, so as to make it possible to defend the inward ramparts and to give orders, from the upper watch, to the men posted in that tower. The middle of that tower, like all those of the outwards walls, except for the barbicans, was covered by a roof, but the embattled watch was under open sky in peace-time and could be provided with covings when there was a siege.

Those permanent roofs rested upon the inward covering of the watch.

The figure 6 gives a plan of that « tour de la Peyre ».

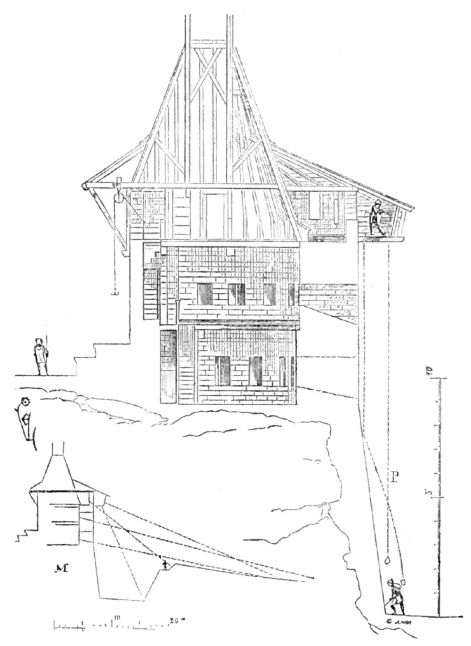

FIGURE 6.

On the point M is sketched a profile of the whole structure with the ditch, the crest-tiles of th counters-carp and the outward ground forming a glacis. We see how the loop-holes are contrived so as to ward off that glacis from razing projectiles and from plunging pro-

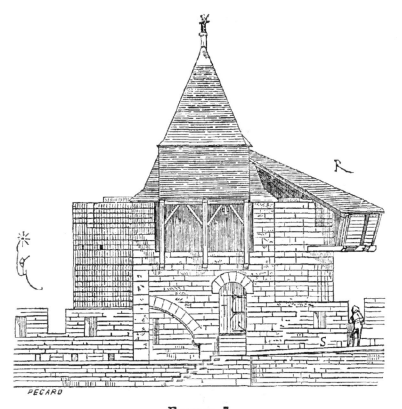

FIGURE 7.

jectiles the crest and foot of the counterscarp. As to the immediate defence, it is assured by the machi-coulis and covings, as is seen on the point P. The figure 7 gives a general sketch of that tower on the inward side, the coving being supposed to be set only on the R side.

Te tower n° 18, called « de la Vade » or « de Pape-

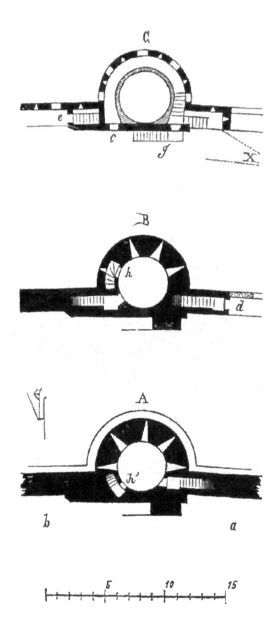

FIGURE 8.

gay » is, although it belongs to the outward walls, is,
as we said, a reduct, a dungeon, commanding all the
table-land on that side, occupied before Saint-Louis's
reign, by a « faubourg ».

The curtains of the outward walls once fallen into
the besiegers' power, most of the towers of those walls
must have been easily taken, for they are scarcely
defended inside and their watches sometimes communicate on a level with those of the curtains; however
some gates interrupt the circulation, but the « tour de
la Vade » is an independent and very high structure;
it possesses two vaulted stories, two stories between
ceilings, a well on the ground-floor, a chimney on the
second story and water-closets on the third. The gate
opening on the lists could be strongly barricaded and
oppose to the besieger an obstacle as resisting as the
walls themselves. The upper story was provided with
battlements under open sky with a roof in the centre.

Those battlements, which, in war-time, were provided with covings, were commanded by the coping of
the tower n° 48.

The other towers of the outward walls are all built
very much on the same model as the tower n° 7, called
« la Porte-Rouge». That tower possesses two stories
under the battlements. The figure 8 gives the plans of
each of those stories. As the ground rises sensibly
from a to b, the two watches of the curtains are not
on the same level; the watch b is at three yards above
the watch a. On the point A is sketched the plan of
the tower under the terre-plein; on B, on the level of
the watch d; on C, on the level of the battlements of
the tower which levels the battlements of the curtain e. We see on d the gate which, opening on the
watch, opens on a staircasse wich goes down to the

lower story A, and, on *e*, the gate which, opening on
the watch, above, opens on a staircase which goes
down to the story B. You reach, from the outside, the
battlements of the tower by the staircase *g*. Moreover,

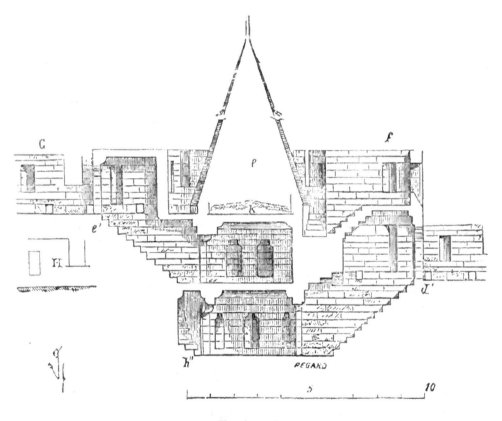

FIGURE 9.

the two stories A and B are set in communication by
an inward staircase *h h'*, taken from the thick of the
wall-tower. Thus the men posted in the two stories A
and B are alone in direct communication with the two
watches of the curtains. If the assailer has succeeded
in destroying the covings and the upper battlements,
and if, thinking to have made the works undefendable,

he attempts to assault one of the curtains, he is receiv-
ed in the flank by posts safety fixed in the lower
stories which, being easily blinded, have not been

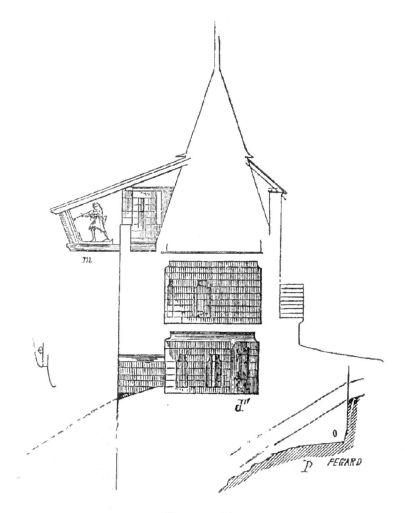

FIGURE 10.

crushed by the stone-engines or made untenable by
the burning of the roof and covings. A longitudinal
section made on the two watches, from *e* to *d*, makes
that disposition clear (fig. 9). We see on the point *e'*

FIGURE 11.

the gate of the staircase *e* and, on *d'* the gate of the staircase *d* of the plan. That last gate is defended by a watch-tower *f*, which is reached by a staircase of six steps. On *h''* begins the staircase which sets in communication the two stories A and B. A layer of earth set on *k* prevents the fire, which might be set to the roof *l* by the besieged, from damaging the upper floor. The figure 10 gives the section of that tower following the perpendicular axis in front. On *d* is the gate opening on the staircase *d*. The covings are set on *m*. On *p* is sketched the profile of the escarpment with the prolongation of the shooting-ranges of the two rows of loop-holes of the stories A and B. It is unnecessary to say that the covings batter the foot *o* of the lower.

A perspective view (fig. 11) taken from the lists (point x of the plan C) will make clear the inward dispositions of that defence.

The stores for the covings and watches of the tower are got, by the battlement *c* of the plan C, by means of a tackle and a pulley, as is shown by the perspective sketch. Here the tower commands only one of the watches (see the section, figure 9). At the time of the construction, under Saint-Louis, it commanded the two curtains; but, under Philip the Bold, when they finished the defence-works of the city, they increased, as has been said before, the relief of some of the curtains of the outward walls which did not seem to have a sufficient outlook. It is then that they raised the battlements G above the older battlements H without taking the trouble of pulling down the latter; so that, on the outside, those first battlemens H remain locked in the raised masonry. Indeed, the outward ground rises like the ground of the lists from *a* to *b* (see the plans) and the engineers, having thought it fit to adopt a uniform outlook of the curtains upon the outside, as well for the outward as for the inward walls, they made all the reliefs regular, in 1285. It must be said, too, that, in those times, they scarcely gave a more important outlook to the towers on the curtains than to the projections, or to some points from which it was useful to command the precincts at a great distance.

As to the large fronts, the flanking towers have, on the curtains, but a feeble outlook, and that disposition also holds good for the large south east side of the outward walls of the city repaired and capped by Philip the Bold.

The disposition of that tower of the outward walls which we have just described is such, that that structure could not defend itself against the outward walls; for, not only is that tower largely commanded, it is, on the side of the lists, wholly undefended.

We have looker over and described the most important points of the two walls of the city. Reverting to the « Porte Narbonnaise » whence we set forth, and ascending to the town through a narrow and winding street we reach, going westward a castle built on the culminating point of the city.

I said that the greater part of the constructions of that citadel dated from the beginning of the XIIth century. The first structure which presents itself on the town-side is a barbican built in the XIIIth century, semi-circular, embatteld, with watches (see the general plan, fig. 16), and in which a front-gate is pierced. That first gate was only defended by loop-holes and leaves, provided with double shutters, a machicoulis and wooden-leaves. It is, as may be seen, a charming construction, well made and tolerably preserved.

9

The wooden-floor and the roofing alone have been done away with, but the trace of those complements is so obvious that their disposition cannot be misunderstood. The upper story of the gate was open on the castle side, so as to prevent the assailers, who might have taken hold of it, from defending themselves against the garrison shut up in the castle. A wide ditch protects three of the fronts of that citadel, the fourth looking on the escarpments which face, the river Aude. A bridge rebuilt in part pretty recently, gave access to the only gate of the castle on the front facing the town. The piers of that bridge date from the XIIIth century and the two last, near the entrance, are disposed in such a way that it must have supported a sliding wooden-floor.

The assailer found a first obstacle formed by a wooden-fence covered with a shed. That obstacle once pulled down, supposing the sliding floor taken off, they had to cross a ditch two yards wide to reach the first portcullis defended by a machicoulis. Behind that portcullis is a wooden-gate a second machicoulis, a second portcullis and a second gate. The second portcullis was worked from the second story, the second from a small room disposed immediately above the passage.

The two towers which flank that entrance include two stories vaulted in an hemispherical calotte, and pierced with loop-holes, the two upper stories are separated by a floor. Those two upper stories, without any partition-walls set the two towers in communication with the space above the passage. It was only possible to reach those stories by a wooden staircase disposed against the flat side of the gate on the yard-side, or by the curtain-watches. The vaulted halls are only

lighted by the loop-holes. The third story gets light
from the yard through a charming romaïc window
with double arches resting on a small marble-column
with a sculpted capital, and also from a very small
opening giving sideways over the entrance outside.
That last window was pierced to allow the besieged
who stood by the first portcullis to see what took place
at the entrance and to take measures in consequence
without unmasking themselves. Although the towers
affect a cyclindric shape outside, inside, the facings of
the upper stories are cantwise. That structure was
evidently meant to make it easy to set the timber of
the roofing. It is musch easier to cut and set timber as
a pavillon on a polygonal than on a circular plan; the
circular plan requires curved boards for the raising-
pieces and, to set the joists, complicated joinings. At
the end of the XIth century they must not have been
very skilful in that sort of constructions which, a century and a half later, had reached such a degree of
perfection; therefore we must not be surprised to see
that shape of pyramidal timber adopted for all the
primitive towers of the castle. The builders compen-
sated the differences in projection produced by the
circular shape of the outward paring by means of
« coyaux ».

The first story communicates with the second by
means of a trap-door opened in the hemispherical
vault. That trap-door, pierced behind the small
window which allows to watch the entrance, was destined to transmit orders to the men who stood by the
second portcullis in the small hall of the first story,
either to drop that portcullis rapidly in case of an
attack or to raise it when a body of men got in; for it
must be noted that the men at the second portcullis

can see what happens outside only through a very narrow loop-hole or through the machicoulis, opened before that second portcullis.

In those defence-works so complete, of which we give the plans figure 12, everything is contrived that orders may come from the top, where the means of defence the most efficient were displayed and where, in consequence, the captain of the tower must have stood at time of the attack.

Our war-ships with their hatchways, their speaking-trumpets and their low batteries can give and idea of the means for transmitting orders then used in fortified works (¹).

All the copings of the walls and towers of the castle reared about the beginning of the XIIth century were defended in war-time by very salient covings, for it will be noticed that the holes trough which passed the swinging boards supporting those covings, are double, pierced at about 0 m. 60 one above the other so as to relieve the upper pieces supporting the floor by small corbels and timber links. The setting of those covings must have been less rapid than that of the XIIIth century covings, supported by strong swingting joists. However, it could be achieved without too much difficulty, supposing the links to be jointed, without any cocking, which, besides, would have been useless since the wooden pieces crossing the walls were perfectly fixed and coud deviate neither to the right nor to the left. A carpenter (fig. 13), astride on the upper

(1) In the figure 12, the transversal section is traced on A. On I is the extremity of the fixed bridge; on B, the ditch covered by a fly-bridge; on C the first portcullis with its windlass on E; on D the second portcullis with its windlass on F; on G the holes of the covings. On H is traced the longitudinal section on the passage and the vaulted hallo.

FIGURE 12.

horizontal joist, could assemble the link sideways with a mallet, taking care to fix it before by means of a bit of rope (²).

The holes of the joists in the battlements of the castle, being smaller than those of the constructions dating from the XIIIth century, explain those additional precautions, destined to prevent the skinging boards from giving way at the extremity. It will be observed, further, that the battlements of the castle are high (2 metres) : that is because the floor of the covings was set at the very foot of those battlements, instead of being set, as in the XIIIth century, at 0 m. 30 above the ground of the watch. It was then necessary to pass through those battlements as through so many gates and give them a sufficient height to enable the defenders to stand in the galleries of the covings.

We must not omit to mention a very curious fact concerning the history of the construction. Most of the gates and windows of the towers of the castle on the yard-side, are coped with lintels in concrete. Those factitious stones have resisted atmospherical influences much better than sandstones; they are composed of perfectly hard mortar mixed with pounded pebbles, large like an egg, and must have

(2) From the watches, the carpenters, slipped into the lower holes a first piece A, then a second swinging piece B. The workman, passing through the battlement, sat astride on that second piece B, as shown by the perspective detail B' then fitted the link C into its joint. The head of that link was joined to the piece B by a peg; a small post D, forced into the system from behind stiffened it all. Thereupon, setting the madriers, it was easy to fix the double posts E between which they slipped the madriers serving as front guard, then they fixed the roofing which covered the coving and the watch so as to shelter the defenders from the projectiles hurled at them. Some notches G, contrived between the madriers, permitted to take aim.

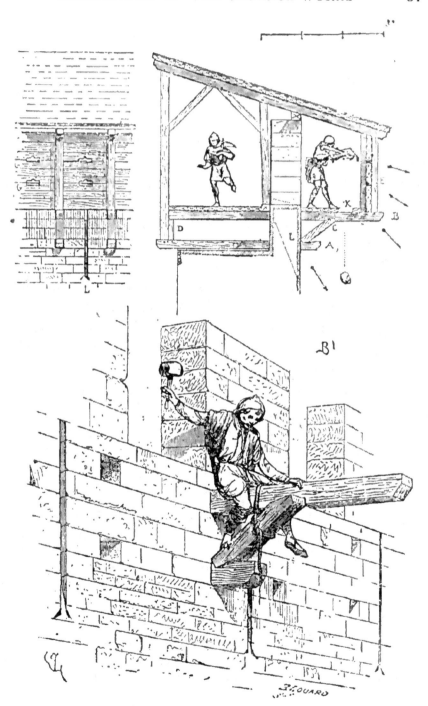

FIGURE 13.

been fashioned in wooden boxes. After having observed on the spot some of those lintels, my attention being roused, I found a pretty large number of those concrete-blocks in the outward restorations of the Visigoth walls undertaken in the XIIth century. It would seem that the builders of the latter period, when they wanted strong materials of comparatively large dimension, made use of that process which proved perfectly successful; for none of those lintels got broken as happened frequently to the stone-lintels.

After passing through the gate of the castle, you come into a spacious yard, surrounder now with modern constructions which have been joined to the curtains and towers. Those structures have been erected on the spot of porticoes dating from the XIIIth century the toothing-stones of which we still find. Traces of fire are apparent on the facings of the XIIth century-constructions and leads us to suppose that those porticoes have replaced wooden-structures lining the yard inside before the restorations undertaken by Louis the IXth and Philip the Bold. On the east and north-sides the walls were lined only by a simple portico. On the south side stands a structure the entire lower part of which dates from the XIIth century and the upper part from the end of the XIIIth with repairrings in the XVth. That building contained, on the ground-floor, kitchens under bent vaults, with a fine semi-circular gate opened in the gable. It separates the large yard from a second one, opening on the south side and closed by a strong XIIth century curtain, completely restored in the XIIIth. To that curtain was joined a structure presenting a very wide portico, on the ground-floor, with a hall on the first story. We

still see, in their places, along the curtain, all the
stone-corbels which supported the floor of that hall,
a fine chimney the profiles and sculptures of which
belong to Saint Louis's time; and, in the angle of the
square tower n° 31, called « tour Peinte », the
toothing-stone of the pillars of the lower portico.
A large square window with mullions lighted, on the
south side, towards Saint-Nazaire, the large hall of
the first story. That window is set above the inward
floor and the disposition of the ceiling which closed
the widening is such that the projectiles flung from
outside could not penetrate into the hall. At the south-
west angle of the castle stand huge structures, sorts
of dungeons or reducts, independent from one another, which commanded the yard and the precints.
The highest but most extensive of those buildings is
the tower called « Peinte » n° 31, which dominates
the whole city of which it was the chief watch-tower.
That tower, on a plan of unequal sides, could contain
and only contained, in fact, one wooden staircase, for
it is not divided, in its entire height by any vault or
floor. A single small romaïc window, pierced about
the middle of its height opens on the country, on the
side of the river Aude. That tower is untouched; we
still see its upper battlements with the holes of the
covings very close to one another, as if to set a salient
outward gallery, fit to resist the terrible winds of the
region.

The plan of the tower n° 35 of the castle, called
« du Major » (one of those of the angle, the other
tower n° 32 being alike), is very interesting to study.
Those two angle-towers are the only ones which
contain spiral staircases, made of stone. The towers
n° 32, 34, 35 and 36 are defended, like the two gate-

towers : the same small halls vaulted in hemispherical calottes, the same disposition of the battlements,
the same combination of pyramidal roofs.

But it is on the west front that a study of the city-
castle is particularly interesting. The west side is
that which looks on the country and faces the large
barbican built at the foot of the escarpment.

To make clear the very complicated dispositions of
that part of the castle, we must get down to the barbican and pass successively through all the windings
so ingeniously combined to make access to the castle
impossible to an armed troop.

Unfortunately the barbican was pulled down about
fifty years ago in order to build a factory along the
river Aude. That destruction is to be for ever regret-
ted, as, according to those who have seen that fine
structure, it produced great effect and was made of
fine materials. I was only able to find, by pretty deep
excavations, its foundations and its first layers, which
only permitted to ascertain exactly its place and
diameter.

The barbican had been reared very probably under
Saint-Louis, like most of the adjunctions and restorations made to the castle. It was pierced with two
rows of loop-holes and was coped by an embattled
watch with covings. It was not covered, its great extent
scarcely allowing of it, but must have possessed inside
wooden galleries making access to the loop-holes easier
and forming a shelter for the defenders.

The gate was pierced in the inward angle, on the
north side, on the flank of the « caponnière » which
ascends to the city (fig. 14) on the point B. That
« caponnière » or slope, fortified on both sides, is
rather narrow at the foot near the barbican. It gets

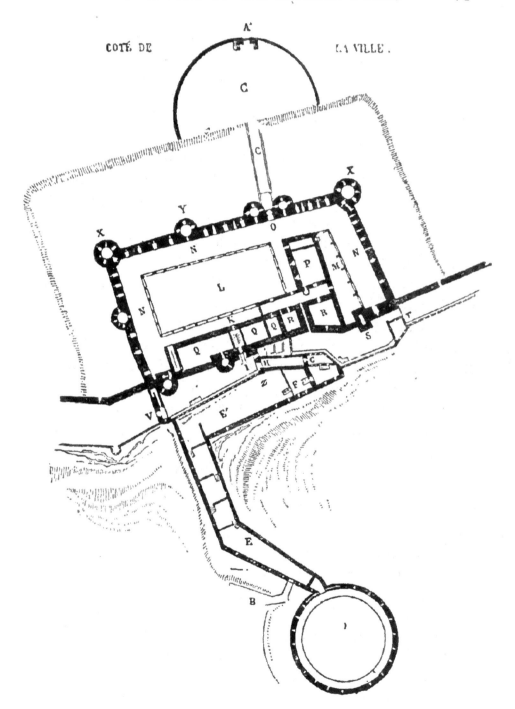

FIGURE 14.

broader on E up to the point where, making a turn, it goes perpendicularly to the front of the castle so as to be enfiladed by the besieged posted on the watches of the double walls, or in the castle itself; then, having reached the foot of the walls, the caponnière winds off on E', to the right, goes along those walls from north to south, to reach a first gate of which only the pilasters are left. Those slopes E are embattled right and left. Their ascent is cut off by overlapping parapets. On F was a watch-wall in front of the first gate; having passed that first gate you had to go along a second watch-wall, to turn off suddenly to the left and find a second gate G, being battered on the flank by the men of the second walls. Then you came to an important and well defended structure; it is a long passage, surmounted with two stories under which you had to pass. The first of those stories battered the gate G and was pierced with machicoulis opening on the passage; the second story was in communication with the upper battlements battering either the slope or the space G. The floor of the second story communicated with the lists only by a narrow gate. If the enemy succeeded in holding that second story, he was caught as if in a mouse-trap for, the small gate closed on him, he found himself exposed to projectiles falling from the machicoulis of the second story; and the extremity of the floor of that first story being broken off on the point H, opposite to the entrance, it was impossible for that assailer to advance. If he succeeded in passing unhindered the passage on the ground-floor he was stopped by the gate H, pierced in a cross-bar coped by the machicoulis of the third story, communicating with the upper watches of the castle. If, against all possibility, the besiegers took hold of the second story, they found no other issus than a small side-gate opening into a hall set on arches, outside the castle, and communicating with the inside only by winding which it was easy to barricade in a moment and which, moreover, were closed by leaves. If, in spite of all those accumulated obstacles, the besiegers forced the third gate H, they had then to attack the postern I of the castle, protected by a system of formidable defence : loop-holes, two machicoulis set one over the other, a bridge with a sliding floor, a portcullis and leaves. Should they have got hold of that gate, they found themselves at 7 metres lower than the inward yard L which was reached only by narrow steps defended, and by passing through several gates on the point K.

Supposing the attack to be pushed through the lists on the side of the « porte de l'Aude », they were stopped by a post I and by a gate with wooden works and a double machicoulis pierced in the floor of an upper story communicating with the large hall N of the castle, by means of a timber-passage which could be destroyed in a moment; so that getting hold of that upper story was no use.

If, after having passed the structure T, they went further on the watch, along the square tower S, they soon came across a watch with a gate duly provided with machicoulis and built perpendicularly to the passage G H After that gate, it wass a third gate, narrow and low, pierced in the big cross-bar Z, which you had to pass; then you reached the postern I of the castle. If, on the contrary, the assailer presented himself on the opposite side, by the north-lists, he was stopped by a defence V, but, on that side, the

attack could not be attempted, for it is the point of
the city best defended by nature. The big cross-bar Z
which, starting from the castle-curtain, pushes for-
ward in a right angle, up to the slope of the barbican,
was coped by transversal machicoulis which commanded the gate H and by an embattled watch-tower
which allowed one to see what happened in the
« caponnière », so as to take inside the necessary
dispositions or to recognize friendly troops ([1]).

That part of the fortifications of the city of Carcassonne is certainly the most interesting; unfortunately it now presents the aspect of a mere ruin. It
is by examining scrupulously the least traces of still
surviving constructions that we can reconstitute those
fine works. I must say, however that few points
remain vague and that the system of defence allows
of no doubt. It tallies exactly with the natural dispositions of the ground and those ruins are still full of
fragments which reveal, not only the disposition of
the stone-constructions, but, moreover, the links, fastenings and sealings of the wooden-structures, of the
floors and defences.

A rough sketch of the castle and barbican restored
which we give further on (fig. 15) shows the whole
of those works.

A plan of the city and town of Carcassonne, taken
in 1774, previous consequently to the destruction of
the barbican, mentions, in the references, a large cave
existing under the « boulevard de la Barbacane » but

---

(1) Our figure 13 shows, on the point C, the barbican on the town-
side with its gate (A'), on O, the castle-gate; on L, the large yard;
on P, the building holding the kitchens; on M, the second yard with
the portico N, which supports the large hall; on Q and R, the buildings, dungeons; on D, the large barbican, and on X, and Y, the
towers of the XIIth century.

FIGURE 15.

filled up long ago. I could find no trace of that construction the existence of which I am very doubtful of.
If that cave ever existed, it must have made the barbican communicate with the fortified mill called « du
Roi » in order to allow the castle-garrison to reach
under shelter the river.

We have calculated the number of men strictly
neccesary to defend the city of Carcassonne.

The outward walls of the city possesses 14
towers; supposing each guarded by 20 men, it
comes to ....   280 men
   Twenty men in each of the three barbicans.   60
To defend the curtains on the points atta-
cked   100
   The inward walls include 24 towers with
20 men for each post; on an average........   480
   For the « Porte Narbonnaise »............   50
   To guard the curtains...................   100
   Fort the castle-garrison   200
                                          1,270

Let us add to that number of men the
captains, one for a post or for a tower, according to the custom.........................   53
                                          1,323

Only the fighting-men are in question here; but we
must add to those numbers the servants, the workmen
needed in great numbers to sustain a siege; that is at
least double the number of the fighting-men. That
number was rigorously sufficient to oppose a sturdy
resistance to the enemy in a place so strongly fortified.

The two walls had not to defend themselves simul-
taneously, and the watchmen in the inward walls
could send off detachments to defend the outward

walls. If these fell into the enemy's power, their defenders took shelter behind the inward walls. Besides, the besieger did not attack all points at the same time. The perimeter of the outward walls is 1400 metres on the curtains; consequently about one fighting man for a yard was needed to constitute the garrison of a fortified town like the city of Carcassonne.

Here are the names of the towers of the two walls referring to the numbers inscribed on the general plan :

OUTWARD WALLS

1. Barbacane de la porte Narbonnaise.
2. Tour de Bérard, also called de Saint-Bernard.
3. Tour de Bénazet.
4. Tour de Notre-Dame, also called de Rigal.
5. Tour de Mouretis.
6. Tour de la Glacière.
7. Tour de la Porte-Rouge.
8. Grande barbacane extérieure du château.
9. Avant-porte de l'Aude.
10. Tour du petit Canizou.
11. Tour de l'Evêque, belonging to the two walls.
12. Tour du grand Canizou.
13. Tour du grand Brulas.
14. Tour d'Ourliac.
15. Tour Crémade, barbacane de la poterne Saint-Nazaire.
16. Tour Cautières.
17. Tour Pouleto.
18. Tour de la Vade, also called du Papegay.
19. Tour de la Peyre.

INWARD WALLS

20. Tours et porte Narbonnaise.
21. Tour du Trésau, also called du Trésor.
22. Tour du moulin du Connétable.
23. Tour du Vieulas.
24. Tour de la Marquière.

25. Tour de Sanson.
26. Tour du moulin d'Avar.
27. Tour de la Charpentière.
37. Tour de la Justice.
38. Tour Visigothe.
39. Tour de l'Inquisition.
40. Tour de Cahuzac.
41. Tour Mipadre, also called tour du Coin ou de Prade.
42. Tour du Moulin.
43. Tour et poterne de Saint-Nazaire.

44. Tour Saint-Martin.
45. Tour des Prisons.
46. Tour de Castera.
47. Tour du Plô.
48. Tour de Balthazar.
49. Tour de Darejean ou de Dareja.
50. Tour Saint-Laurent.
51. Staircase going down to the postern of the tour de la Peyre.
52. Tour du Trauquet.
53. Tour de Saint-Sernin.

CASTLE

28. Tour de la Chapelle.
29. Tour de la Poudre.
30. Avant-porte du château.
31. Tour Peinte. Guette.
32. Tour Saint-Paul.

33. Porte du château.
34. Tour des Casernes.
35. Tour du Major.
36. Tour du Degré.
54. Barbacane intérieure du château.

THE SAINT-NAZAIRE CHURCH

Formely the Cathedral

That church is composed of a nave the construction
of which dates from the end of the XIth century or
the beginning of the XIIth, and of a transept with an
absis and chapels dating from the beginning of the
XIVth century.

We shall not undertake to discuss on the edifices
which may have preceeded the church we see nowadays and the oldest parts of which date no further
than the year 1090. We shall not try either to analyse
the motives which led to the reconstruction of the
chancel, the transept and the chapels in the beginning
of the XIVth century, historical documents being
absolutely lacking. But a certain fact is that those
XIVth century structures have been raised on those
romaïc foundations which have been found everywhere, and more particularly in the XIth century-
crypt which we found out under the chancel in 1857,
and which was then cleared off. The vaults of that
crypt alone had been destroyed in order to lower the
ground of that chancel in the XIVth century. They
were replaced by a stone-ceiling which leaves us
glimpses of the old pillars and walls pierced with
small bays.

The romaïc nave presents a disposition which has
been adopted pretty frequently in the churches of
Provence and Bas-Languedoc. The central vault, with
arch-wise joist is buttressed by vaults equally arch-
wise opening the very narrow aisles. That nave then

is only lighted by the windows of the side-walls.
A semi-circular gate dating from the beginning of the
XIIth century is opened in the north-aisle for, in
older times, the west front of the nave, as we said
before, was near the ramparts and contributed to
defending them. Its foot was only pierced with a very
small gate which opened into a passage the toothing-
stones of which we still perceive.

About 1260 they joined to the south flank of the
romaïc transept a chapel the floor of which is on the
level of the pavement of the old cloister that is to
say about two yards above the church-ground. That
chapel contains the tomb of Bishop Radulphe the inscription of which gives the date 1266 as being that
of the prelate's death. It is on the supplications of
that bishop that the inhabitants of the faubourgs
of the city, banished in consequence of the siege
undertaken by Viscount Raymond de Trincavel,
were authorized to re-build their town on the
other bank of the Aude. That tomb is a very interesting monument although the figure of the personage
executed in basso-relievo, is mediocre; the image of
the sarcophagus which supports it, gives a series of
small figures perfectly preserved, representing the
canons of the cathedral in their choir-garb. That
basement is intact, for the ground of the chapel having
been raised up to the level of that the transept, the
lower parts of the monument remained buried for
centuries and have thus been preserved from muti-
lations. The choir, the transept and the chapels have
been erected under the bishopric of Pierre de Roquefort, from 1300 to 1320. The romaïc plan has been
adopted in the construction of that part of the church,
and that is why the two wings of that transept present

an original disposition which belongs only to a few edifices of the romaïc school of the South, previous to the XIIIth century.

Indeed, on each of those cross-aisles open three chapels set towards the east, separated only by openings above blind basement-arcades. Four of the pillars which form the separation of those chapels are cylindric, as if to recall those of the XIIth century-nave.

The bishop Pierre de Roquefort seemed to intend to make if his Saint-Nazaire-cathedral, so modest in extent, a master-piece of elegance and richness. Contrary to what we see at Narbonne, where sculpture is entirely lacking, ornaments are lavished in Saint-Nazaire-church. The windows, immense and numerous (for that apsis and that transept seem a regular lantern), are truly magnificent in composition and colour. The chancel, the pillars of which are decorated with statues of the apostles, was entirely painted. The two side-chapels of the extremity of the nave, to the north and south, were probably erected only after the death of Pierre de Roquefort, for they are not related to the transept as to construction and in one of them, the north one, is placed, not subsequently, the tomb of that bishop, one of the most graceful monuments of the XIVth century that we know.

The strong south-east and west winds which reign at Carcassonne had caused the chief gate to be opened on the north flank of the romaïc nave; another gate is pierced in the gable of the north-cross-aisle; and in the angle of that cross-aisle is a pretty staircase shaped as a salient small tower. On the two sides of the chancel between the counterforts are disposed two small sacrariums which go only up to the window-tills. Those sacrariums are provided with double closets, strongly iron-bound and taken from the thick of the walls. They served as treasury, for it was the custom to place on each side of the grand altar of abbey-churches or cathedrals, closets destined to contain the sacred vases, deliquaries and all precious objects.

Besides the tombs of the bishops Radulphe and Pierre de Roquefort we see, on the walls of the chancel, on the gospelside, a fine alabaster-tomb of a bishop whose statue is lying on a sarchophagus and who is said to be Simon Vigor, archbishop of Narbonne, who died at Carcassonne in 1575. That tomb and the statue dating from the XIVth century cannot, in consequence, be ascribed to that prelate. We shall point out another mistake. A funeral slab was laid in Saint-Nazaire-church which is supposed to have belonged to the tomb of the famous Simon de Montfort. Firstly the tomb of Simon de Montfort was erected near Montfort-l'Amaury, in the church of the abbey of « Hautes-Bruyères », and if there ever was, at Carcassonne, a monument erected to his memory, after the raising of the siege of Toulouse, it could only be a funeral slab. Then the engraving of that slab, the inscription are wrought by an ignorant and unskilled forger. However that slab having been found, it appears, without any one knowing exactly where or how, and presented to Saint-Nazaire-church, we did not think it right to reject it.

We see, inlaid into the wall of the chapel on the right, a fragment of a basso-relievo, of greater interest because it represents the attack of a fortified place. That fragment, though very roughly wrought, dates from the first half of the XIIIth century. The assailer tries to force the lists of a town surrounded with walls and the besieged work a mangonel. They saw in that basso-relievo a representation of the death of Simon de Montfort, killed before the walls of Toulouse by the stone of an engine worked by women on the « place de Saint-Sernin ». The supposition is not improbable, that basso-relievo dating from the time of that siege and angels carrying away up into the skies the soul of a personage, in human shape, which may well be that of Simon de Montfort.

Among the finest glass-frames which decorate the windows of the Saint-Nazaire-cathedral, we must mention that of the first chapel near the chancel, on the epistleside, which represents Christ on the cross, with the temptation of Adam, prophets holding phylacteries on which are written the prophecies relative to the coming and death of the Messiah. That window is one of the most remarkable of the XIVth century for skill in harmonizing the colours. But, in the chancel, there exist two windows supplied, in the XVIth century, with glass-frames of great value which belong to the fine « Ecole toulousaine » of the Renaissance. The « grisailles » are modern and have been fabricated with the help of old fragments still subsisting. The glass-frames of the two rose-windows and of the two chapels of the nave are old and have simply been restored with the utmost care.

The vestry, joined to the chapel of Bishop Radulphe has been built at the same time as that chapel, then repaired in the XVth century.

THE CITY INSIDE

There exist, inside the city, only a few fragments of the old houses and three wells. One, broad, with a fine brink surmounted with three pillars dating from the XIVth century. That well has been dug in the rock at a very early time, and is filled up now; the other, much narrower the brink of which dates from the XVth century, the third in the cloister of Saint-Nazaire. There must have existed cisterns in the city, for those three wells and those dug in some of the towers, as has been seen, could not supply sufficiently the wants of the garrison and of the inhabitants. A single one of those cisterns has been discovered by us; it is dug under the slope of the « porte de l'Aude » between the two walls. You get down to it by a stair-case, contrived in the thick of the first walls, and they could draw up the water it contained by a draft-hole with a brink which we see along that wall on going up to the « porte de l'Aude ». That cistern is now partly filled up; it must have been supplied by the rainwater collected between the « porte de l'Aude » and the cloister of Saint-Nazaire, and perhaps by a spring which gives now very little water.

We still see, joined to the inward ramparts, buildings which have been reared at the same time as the defence-works and were probably destined to contain posts and superior commanders. Those remains, are apparent : on the « porte Narbonnaise » — inward side on the left, behind the towers n°ˢ 51, 52, 48, and 44, inside the « porte de l'Aude » and behind the tower n° 25.

A small church existed along the walls, near the « Porte Narbonnaise »; it was the church of Saint-Sernin, the apsis of which was formed by the tower n° 53. In the XVth century, a window with mullions was opened in that apsis, through the Visigoth masonry. The church was pulled down during the last century; it was of Romaïc structure.

This brief description of the city of Carcassonne can make us understand the importance of those remains, the interest they present, and how capital it was not to let them perish. The church of Saint-Nazaire has been completely restored by the care of the « Commission des Monuments historiques ». Those works, undertaken in 1844, were only finished in 1860. All the towers of the inward walls, discovered long ago, and particularly the vaulted ones, had suffered much from the rigours of the atmosphere. Those ruins have long been given up to the inhabitants of the city who did not scruple to take away the materials of the parapets and of the watches within their reach and to use the towers to deposit their filth. To circulate on the watch was very difficult. On the south front, a large number of houses and hovels still leant on the ramparts. Those houses which constitute what is still called to-day « Quartier des Lices », are occupied by a poor population of weavers who live on damp ground-floors, huddled with tame animals.

Since 1855, works of restoration and especially of consolidation and covering of the towers have been undertaken in the city of Carcassonne under the high supervision of the « Commission des Monuments historiques ».

Every year, since that time, loans are made to restore the parts of the walls which suffer most and present most interest. Already most of the towers of the inward walls are covered as they used to be. Bits of wall which threatened ruin, especially about the « porte de l'Aude » have been re-set and consolidated, the watches are practicable. On his part, the war-administration has put some money at our disposal, and, every year, the « Conseil Général de l'Aude » and the town of Carcassonne grant sums which are specially affected to acquiring the houses still leaning on the ramparts.

Although the sums disponible are not great every year yet the result obtained is considerable and the many strangers who visit nowadays the city of Carcassonne can form an accurate idea of the system of defence employed in the fortifications of the diverse periods of the Middle Ages.

I do not know, in the whole of Europe, of such complete and formidable works of the VIth, XIIth and XIIIth centuries, a subject of study so interesting, a more picturesque site. All those who care for old monuments who love and know the history of our country wish to see that restoration completed and, already in the south, the city of Carcassonne, scarcely visited formerly, has become a resort for all travellers.

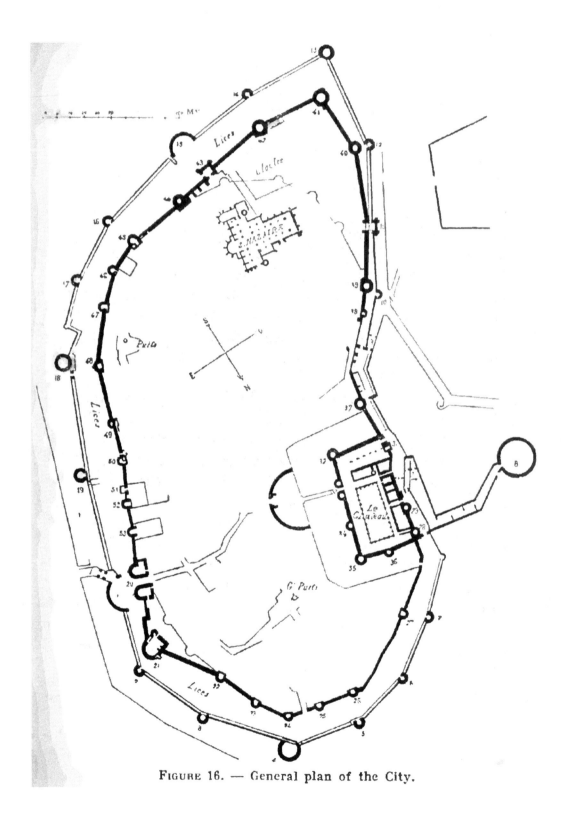

FIGURE 16. — General plan of the City.

DOCUMENTS D'ART

Collection d'ouvrages d'amateur in-4° (18 × 24) comportant un texte et un album de planches en portefeuille. La série se vend également reliée demi-chagrin, tête dorée, moyennant un supplément de 5o fr. par volume.

MUSÉE DU LOUVRE

Le Mobilier Français, par Carle DREYFUS, conservateur-adjoint au Musée du Louvre.

   I. *Époques de Louis XIV et de Louis XV*, 41 planches.

   II. *Époque de Louis XVI*, 51 planches.

     Les deux albums ensemble........................ **120 fr.**

Les Objets d'Art du XVIIIᵉ siècle, par Carle DREYFUS, conservateur-adjoint au Musée du Louvre.

   I. *Époque de Louis XV*, 25 planches.

   II. *Époque de Louis XVI*, 41 planches.

     Les deux albums ensemble........................ **90 fr.**

La Céramique Française, par Mˡˡᵉ M.-J. BALLOT, attachée au Musée du Louvre.

   I. *Bernard Palissy et les fabriques du XVIᵉ siècle.*

     Un album de 48 planches, dont 25 en couleurs, et 46 pages de texte.

   II. *Nevers, Rouen et les fabriques des XVIIᵉ et XVIIIᵉ siècles.*

     Un album de 48 planches, dont 36 en couleurs, et 52 pages de texte.
     Les deux albums ensemble........................ **200 fr.**

La Céramique Chinoise, par J.-J. MARQUET DE VASSELOT, conservateur-adjoint et Mˡˡᵉ M.-J. BALLOT, attachée au Musée du Louvre.

     Deux albums de planches et texte, avec les fac-similés exacts des marques des potiers et des fabriques.

   I. *De l'époque des Han à l'époque des Ming (2o6 avant J.-C.-1643).*

     Un album de 40 planches, dont 28 en couleurs.

   II. *De l'époque de K'ang-Hi à nos jours (1662-1911).*

     Un album de 44 planches, dont 32 en couleurs.
     Les deux albums ensemble........................ **200 fr.**

L'Art Chinois. Sculptures, Bronzes, Orfèvrerie, Fer, Peinture, par Gaston MIGEON, directeur honoraire des Musées Nationaux.

     Un album de 58 planches, dont 6 en couleurs, et 40 pages de texte .... **90 fr.**

*

L'Orient Musulman, par Gaston MIGEON, directeur honoraire des Musées Nationaux.

I. *Sculptures de pierre et de bois, ivoires, armes, bronzes et cuivres, tapis et tissus, miniatures.*
Un album de 52 planches, dont 6 en couleurs.

II. *Cristaux de roche, verres émaillés, céramiques.*
Un album de 51 planches, dont 20 en couleurs.
Les deux albums ensemble........................ 200 fr.

La Céramique Japonaise, par Mlle M.-J. BALLOT, attachée au Musée du Louvre.
Un album de 46 planches, dont 12 en couleurs....... 100 fr.

L'Estampe Japonaise, par Gaston MIGEON, directeur honoraire des Musées Nationaux.

I. *XVIIe et XVIIIe siècles.*
Un album de 36 planches dont 13 en couleurs.

II. *XVIIIe et XIXe siècles.*
Un album de 39 planches, dont 23 en couleurs.
Les deux albums ensemble........................ 180 fr.

L'Art Japonais. Sculpture de bois, peintures, laques, poteries, armes et étuis, bronzes, gardes de sabre, par Gaston MIGEON, directeur honoraire des Musées Nationaux.
Un album de 60 planches, dont 7 en couleurs......... 90 fr.

Antiquités Orientales. Sumer, Babylonie, Élam, par J. CONTENAU, attaché au Musée du Louvre.
Un album de 54 planches........................ 70 fr.

Les Pastels du XVIIe et du XVIIIe siècle, par P. RATOUIS DE LIMAY, archiviste au Ministère des Beaux-Arts.
Un album de 60 planches, dont 12 en couleurs....... 100 fr.

Les Dessins de Michel-Ange, par Louis DEMONTS.
Un album de 18 planches, avec catalogue raisonné.... 30 fr.

Les Dessins de Léonard de Vinci, par Louis DEMONTS.
Un album de 26 planches, avec catalogue raisonné.... 35 fr.

Les Dessins de Claude Gellée, dit *Le Lorrain,* par Louis DEMONTS.
Un album de 56 planches, avec introduction et catalogue descriptif .... 70 fr.

Dessins italiens du XVIIe siècle, par Gabriel ROUCHÈS.
Un album de 36 planches et 20 pages de texte........ 50 fr.

Prud'hon, peintures, pastels et dessins, par Jean GUIFFREY, conservateur au Musée du Louvre.
Un album de 47 planches........................ 70 fr.

ÉDITIONS ALBERT MORANCÉ

DOCUMENTS
ET SOUVENIRS

Le Théâtre de la rue, par PAUL GINISTY.

> Un album in-4° (18×24) de 64 pages de texte et 24 planches, dont 1 en couleurs, en portefeuille.................... 50 fr.

Le Théâtre romantique, par PAUL GINISTY.

> Un album in-4° (18×24) de 50 pages de texte historique, et de 46 planches documentaires, dont 6 en couleurs, sous élégant porte-feuille .... 75 fr.

Le Berry de George Sand, par AURORE SAND.

> Un volume in-4° (18×24) de 192 pages de texte, illustré de 10 dessins dans le texte et 12 hors-texte en héliotypie, broché sous couverture romantique .... 50 fr.
> Il a été tiré 25 exemplaires sur hollande Van Gelder.. 150 fr.

Louis XV intime, par CLAUDE SAINT-ANDRÉ.

> Un bel album in-4° (18×24) de 72 pages de texte, décorées de bandeaux et culs-de-lampe, et 40 planches en héliotypie, dont 7 en couleurs, sous portefeuille de luxe............... 75 fr.

L'Impératrice Eugénie, par LACOUR-GAYET, Membre de l'Institut.

> Un bel album in-4° (18×24) de 104 pages de texte et 40 planches en héliotypie, dont 1 en couleurs, sous portefeuille de luxe. 75 fr.
> Il a été tiré 25 exemplaires sur hollande Van Gelder.. 150 fr.

Le Palais du Louvre, par HENRI VERNE, Directeur des Musées Nationaux et de l'École du Louvre.

I. — *Comment il a grandi de Philippe-Auguste à Louis XIV.*
II. — *Comment l'ont terminé Louis XIV, Napoléon Ier et Napoléon III.*

> Deux albums in-4° (18×24) de 92 pages de texte et 86 planches, dont 11 en couleurs, présentés sous portefeuilles de luxe. 130 fr.

ÉDITIONS ALBERT MORANCÉ

Le Prix des Estampes
Anciennes et Modernes

Par Lucien MONOD

PRIX ATTEINTS DANS LES VENTES
SUITES ET ÉTATS, BIOGRAPHIES ET BIBLIOGRAPHIES

Cet ouvrage est devenu le livre de chevet de tous les amateurs et marchands d'estampes. Il donne par ordre alphabétique des noms d'auteurs, la liste complète des œuvres de tous les graveurs anciens et contemporains, français et étrangers, avec indication des prix atteints dans les ventes, les suites et états et les renseignements biographiques et bibliographiques concernant chaque artiste. C'est un travail d'une importance unique dans cet ordre d'idées, car il réunit, dans l'essentiel, toutes les connaissances iconographiques et monographiques dispersées jusqu'ici dans une foule d'ouvrages rares et onéreux.

Cette Encyclopédie de l'Estampe comprendra
huit volumes in-8 brochés
Sept volumes sont parus (lettres A à S)
Le huitième est sous presse
Chaque volume. . . . . . . **35 francs**

ÉDITIONS ALBERT MORANCÉ
A PARIS, 30 ET 32, RUE DE FLEURUS

CPSIA information can be obtained
at www.ICGtesting.com
Printed in the USA
BVHW011735291018
531563BV00011B/193/P